Other Books by Dr. Bill Miller

Ministry:

Narrow is the Gate: An Introduction to the Christian Religion
Spirit Led Christian
The New Testament Tithe
Prosperity School...Straight from the Bible

History:

The Influence of Christianity on Early Texas History

Christianity and Politics:

The Truth about Open Borders

Financial Teaching Books:

Employee to Employer in 90 Days
Start a Home Business in 30 Days
Credit Repair that Reduces Monthly Payments
Budget Yourself to Financial Victory
Debt Smashdown: Payment Strategies that Succeed
Life Changing Financial Principles...Straight from the Bible

Church Administration (out of print):

Policy Administration in the Local Church
A Generic Policy Manual for the Local Church
Deacon Operating and Policy Manual
Policy Manual for the Children's Ministry
New Members Teaching Guide for the Local Church

AN INAUSPICIOUS HERO
The Story of Sumner Bacon

Dr. Bill Miller

MAKE A WAY® MINISTRIES INC

An Inauspicious Hero...The Story of Sumner Bacon
Copyright © April 2016 by Rev. William Miller
Updates and Re-edits: December 2016, December 2020

MAKE A WAY® PUBLISHING
Miami, Florida

Mailing Address:
P.O. Box 1164
Granbury, Texas 76048

1-800-357-4223

www.makeaway.net
www.creditcounseling.net

ISBN: 13-978-1536962864
ISBN: 1536962864

CONTENT

ACKNOWLEDGMENTS

With thanks and great affection to the Board of Directors of the *Texas Heroes Foundation* in Granbury Texas for their encouragement and for the gift of allowing my wife and me to be involved in their activities. They bought into the idea that Texas History isn't complete without finding out what God was doing while all that history was under construction which was really encouraging.

Also, with much appreciation to my wife Sherri who knows how much I enjoy writing things and loves me anyway even though I am compelled to tell her each and every day in exhaustive detail everything I just learned about my current subject...over and over again. Please pray for Sherri.

And, with great regard as well to the Presbyterian Church that played such an important role in the development of the Texas Territory and encouraged Rev. Sumner Bacon to come among us. I sincerely recommend that as many Presbyterians as possible celebrate one of our real Texas heroes who WELL represented them with all his heart.

Many thanks to my faithful proof readers in reverse alphabetical order: Rev. Glenn Ward, Lana Robinson and Sherri Miller. They were busy with other things but made time available to help bring this little book to its conclusion.

Finally, in Chapter Five I had the fun of telling some of the famous Sumner Bacon legends. Unless otherwise indicated in that chapter, I used as the primary reference source a book called *"Pistol Packing Preachers"* by Barbara Barton. It's a wonderful book about Texas history and I recommend it. I bought it and have it parked in my Barnes and Noble Nook for future reference. I'm indebted to Mrs. Barton for the inspiration of her book and thoroughly enjoyed her folksy way of storytelling.

ROCK SPRINGS PRESBYTERIAN CHURCH

Rock Springs Presbyterian Church is the oldest continuing Protestant church in Texas. It is located in northwestern Nacogdoches County and was originally inspired as an illegal home Bible study by Rev. Sumner Bacon in 1834. It became a beacon of hope during the turmoil of the Texas Revolution at a time when Indian attacks were not uncommon and when Protestant worship was forbidden by Mexican law. The church was originally known as the Watkins Settlement Presbyterian Church named after its founding Pastor, Richard Overton Watkins.

INTRODUCTION

Several years ago, we became involved in a local nonprofit organization called the *Texas Heroes Foundation* that focuses on encouraging the public's awareness of Texas history, especially among young people. To be sure, Texas has a rich history to be proud of and we're known for talking about it and celebrating it at the drop of a ten-gallon hat. Just mention the word *ALAMO* to a native Texan and get ready to *"set a spell"* because that may be the last word you get in for quite a while.

I enjoy learning about Texas history, a lot. I'm a native Texan and I live presently in the special little *historic* town of Granbury, Texas. That means I'm in possession of a certain number of Texas genes (I'm not sure how many) that have pre-programmed me to be interested in the history here. In fact, I'm pretty much defenseless in the face of so much of it to find out and write about.

Nevertheless, as an ordained minister, I discovered that I wanted to know more about what the *Body of Christ* was doing while all that Texas history was going through its early birth pangs. So, I wound up writing a book called *"The Influence of Christianity on Early Texas History"* and in doing that I learned that God had a whole plan going on that for some reason the regular historians hardly ever talk about.

While researching that first book, I ran across a colorful character by the name of Rev. Sumner Bacon, a determined evangelist who came into Texas without any church credentials in order to preach the gospel illegally to whoever would listen while keeping at the ready a loaded six gun in case any trouble makers showed up that didn't like the message. And in addition to all that, he knew James Bowie and Sam Houston personally, was at ground zero and fully involved in the Texas Revolution at the highest levels, and was personally responsible for starting one of the major Church Denominations in Texas that was a key part of our early development.

I want to warn you ahead of time that I've introduced a couple of ideas into this book that don't quite agree with some of our most credible historians. I think I've got it right but so do they and we'll have to wait for more info to surface or for Jesus to explain it to us. I've called attention to these differences during my telling of the story and you be the judge. I'm not exactly an expert but I found some compelling documentation that led me to the characterizations I made about this special minister particularly during the years before he finally became a believer.

I have included a lot of interesting information in the five appendixes and I encourage you to read them instead of just reading the narrative of the Sumner Bacon story. It all connects together and you will come away from this book with a more complete idea of life in Texas during the first four decades of the 19th Century.

Finally, I hope you enjoy getting to know one of our really special Texas characters. His kind helped us become who we are today: tough, determined and sometimes when necessary as ornery as one of those wild, open-range longhorns of days gone by.

Dr. Bill Miller
April 2016

Rev. Sumner Bacon

PROLOGUE

The first time I laid eyes on the Rev. Sumner Bacon he was wearing buckskins and a hunting shirt, and riding an old tired looking gray horse into the dusty little Texas town I'd just arrived in a couple a hours earlier. Coming along behind him was another run-down pony with what looked to me like a lot of trail supplies all tied up some kinda way. Later on, I found out that what he was carrying on that pack horse was mostly bibles he'd wrapped up in a bear skin.

Some of the town folks was saying he was a preacher man they'd got to know from a previous visit the year before. It seems he'd come to town to share the Word of God with whoever would take the time to come listen to what he had to say. They told me it was pretty much all he ever talked about but that he spoke it in a way you could understand. After he'd left town, the illegal bible study group some of them went to on Sunday mornings had grown so much they had to find a bigger place to meet at.

My first thought about him was that he looked like a wilderness man, like somebody who makes his living trapping wild animals out in the woods someplace. But there was also something kinda special about him that made you want to take a second look. He passed right in front of me that day on his way to the *Public Bath House* and looked me straight in the eye as he was a-passing by. The thing that got my notice was that his eyes seemed to flash light in some kinda way. It was like them eyes a-his was talking to me and saying: "I know something special you need to know but you'll have to come out and set a spell so I can explain it to you. If you do, it will change your life."

The rest of him was kinda average. He had, you might say, regular darkish features with a mess of jet-black hair falling almost to his shoulders, in disorder that day more than usual because of exposure to the weather. Also, I noticed he was really tan and wiry looking as if he was used to working hard outdoors. He was about average size but tough looking like you'd want to take some help with you if you was going to go confront him about something important.

He also wore a big six shooter holstered outside his buckskins and just by looking at him you could tell he knew how to use it. Later on, I found out it was mostly for show and that he carried it mainly to discourage the folks who didn't want him preaching. It was also for scaring off Indians when they tried to come around his campsite, but it was said he didn't shoot them neither.

As I think about it now, the most noticeable thing about old Sumner was the way he carried hisself. He seemed to give off this confidence like he was at peace with everything and knew if he could get a chance to talk to you, he could convince you to do whatever he wanted. And, you'd want to do it because you understood it was just the right thing to do.

I heard tell he'd been through some hard times and that it was a constant fight trying to preach the Word of God on the go all the time because there was so many people who didn't want him preaching. But he was always happy about what he was doing with a smile on his face, and you just knew there was no problem old Sumner would ever face that he wouldn't come out on top.

That first evening, I decided to go hear his preaching. The town folk told me he got all excited about what he was saying and put on quite a show. I didn't have nothing else to do 'cept go to the saloon so I decided I could go hear the preaching for a while and go to the saloon later. I didn't plan on being in that town long anyways and I might not run across Rev. Bacon again for quite a spell.

His meeting was held outdoors in a clearing off the main road about a mile out of town. Somebody had made their place available and I noticed some extra-sized hombres posted around the perimeter of the clearing, armed and looking really serious. By the time Sumner showed up, there was more than a hundred fifty people there and only God Hisself knows where they all come from. I sure hadn't seen that many back in the little town.

Soon the Reverend started preaching. It was summer so the sun was still up and it was mighty hot. But after just a few minutes, the heat didn't matter no more because I was already hearing some things I'd never known about before. At least two hours went by before I give it another thought with this man a God speaking all that time so strong about Jesus, I didn't want him to stop. I'd forgotten about the saloon too 'cause I'd become totally concentrated on the man's preaching.

After quite a spell he come to the end of his talk and was inviting people to make a public declaring of their belief in Christ and get prayed over up at the front area where he'd been a-preaching. Suddenly there come this strange feeling going through my body. Something on the inside had come alive like a fire and I felt like I just had to go up there where he was waiting. Everything they'd told me about him was true. At the time, I thought it was his speaking that was pulling at me. But come to find out later on, it was the Holy Spirit working through him that drew me out that night into another life.

The Reverend hisself prayed over me there on the spot in front of everbody. And he prayed really loud, and long. When he'd finished, he give me a Bible and told me to start reading it every day 'cause it would change my life. Ever since then, I've tried to do what he told me and it's worked out like he said. That Bible a his has helped me be somebody I never thought possible.

He stayed in town almost that entire week and I went to hear him speak ever evening each time in a different place. Over them extra days, I got to know him and found out he's somebody mighty special. By the end of his stay, it seemed like we was old friends and I was genuinely sorry when it come time to go our own ways. After he'd left town that last day, the *federales* showed up looking for him, but nobody knew where he'd gone off to. Or they wasn't saying if maybe they did know.

That was ten year ago back in the summer of '34 and now I hear tell the Reverend ain't feeling so good. I wish I had some kinda way to let him know how much I owe him and how grateful I am we met up that time when him and the Lord showed up and changed my life.

Testimony of a composite Texian convert under Sumner Bacon
Early January 1844
Republic of Texas

(Text corrected for most grammar and spelling mistakes, but it still ain't quite perfect)

Do not despise these small beginnings, for the LORD rejoices to see the work begin…

Zechariah 4:10
Living Bible

ONE: A FAR DISTANT BEGINNING

In the state of Texas there are so many heroes in our history that once in a while we still find some new ones. In fact, this book is about a special character I came across a couple of years ago when I was researching another project. The more I read about him, the more obvious it became that his impressive achievements far exceeded his reputation. As an ordained minister and part time history buff, I'm especially interested in the influence Christianity has had on the development of our history so I'm naturally on the lookout for special people of God that have been overlooked. Eventually I felt a special calling to tell the story of the Rev. Sumner Bacon from San Augustine, Texas.

I was first drawn to him by a picture I found on the Internet showing a neatly trimmed-out minister holding a revolver in one hand and a bible in the other. His expression suggests he was using that moment to make clear he didn't want folks thinking he was just some typical country preacher. It's not really so unusual to find 19th century photos and paintings of authentic Texas heroes holding firearms. But at the time this particular picture was made, the ruggedly handsome face looking back at us with six-shooter prominently displayed belonged to a seriously dedicated and widely traveled Evangelist who had become a key figure in the development of Texas.

As I looked a little more into this gun-toting minister's life, I found out that he'd faced some significant challenges on his way to that day of posing for the picture. It's interesting that so many of our heroes achieve their special status after having to overcome a beginning so full of hardships that what comes later seems impossible for the majority of us to have successfully dealt with. In the case of young Sumner Bacon, it took the Creator God of the Universe to personally turn the impossibilities in his life into something special so that His intricate plan for the development of Texas could be fully implemented.

The fact is though, when you study your Bible, you'll find all the way through it that a lot of God's heroes have followed similarly impossible paths before eventually arriving at the destiny He had designed for them. And, what the Bible actually reveals through that model is that God seems to prefer doing things that way so that when we see that something really special has happened, we'll know for certain He's the One that made it all possible. That's exactly how the story developed for young Sumner Bacon because looking back at it, only God could have pulled it all off.

The Beginning

Now the word *inauspicious* in the title of this book seems to fit this newly found hero of ours to a tee. The meaning of it is *unpromising* or *unlikely* and that was how young Sumner started off in life: it was *unlikely* according to most standards of predicting things that he would ever amount to much. And during the first part of *his* life, he seemed bound and determined to take advantage of every opportunity to confirm for folks that a low opinion of him would be well deserved.

The first thing our future Texas hero would have to overcome was that he was born in Massachusetts. Nothing against Massachusetts, but in those horse and buggy days, it was a really long way from there to Texas. And even that got a little mixed up because historians say he was born in the town of Auburn but it wasn't even called Auburn until 1837 which was forty-seven years *after* Sumner was born. So, to be totally accurate about it, Sumner Bacon was born in Ward, Massachusetts on January 22, 1790.

And just so you know the rest of that little story, the town of Ward was incorporated in 1778 at the height of the Revolutionary War and was named after the American Major General Artemas Ward. But it seems the United States Post Office was having trouble with the fact that the name was too close in spelling to the nearby town of Ware, named in 1775 after a town of the same name in England,[1] and so prevailed upon the leadership of Ward to change their name. After an extensive confrontation about it, the name was finally changed to Auburn and it's been that way ever since[2] even though General Ward was elected twice to the U.S. House of Representatives after the War and was a man of great prominence all through that area.[3] Apparently the U.S. Post Office already knew how to use its federal power even though the country was scarcely 50 years old!

But to get back to our story, young Sumner was welcomed into the world by his proud parents Jonathan and Molly Adams Bacon as the year 1790 was getting underway.[4] There were two older siblings: Jonathan (b. 1784) named after his father and Betsy (b. 1786) making Sumner the youngest of the family's three children.

---

[1] https://en.wikipedia.org/wiki/Ware,_Massachusetts
[2] https://en.wikipedia.org/wiki/Auburn,_Massachusetts
[3] https://en.wikipedia.org/wiki/Artemas_Ward
[4] https://tshaonline.org/handbook/online/articles/fba03

Now as the story develops, you'll need to keep in mind that the historical documentation of this little family is a bit sketchy especially in Sumner's early years. One thing we *do* know is that the father was reputed to be a jovial, good natured individual who was fun to be around but for some reason relatively unsuccessful in his business dealings.[5] The family would most likely have attended a local *Puritan* church in Ward and been a part of their small farming community because that's the pattern that can be documented in their next location.

In 1804 the family moved away from Ward and headed west to seek something new on another small farm, all the way to Greenfield, Massachusetts (about 70 miles to the NW) which at the time was still sort of frontier territory, at least by New England standards. It's said that the original family plan was for Sumner to become an attorney,[6] a person of respect who could've lifted the family out of the mediocre pattern of life they'd become accustomed to. For some reason that plan never happened which explains in part the sketchiness of their early history: they just weren't prominent enough for the record keepers to take note of. As if to confirm their lack of prominence, their Puritan Church in Greenfield, called the *North Parish Congregation,* specifically notes in its history that the Bacon Family pew was located in the very back of the church sanctuary.[7]

It's interesting as well that the sketchy historical record also reveals that the older brother Jonathan followed in his father's footsteps and had difficulty in his business

---

[5] http://www.genealogy.com/forum/surnames/topics/bacon/4017/
[6] https://tshaonline.org/handbook/online/articles/fba03
[7] http://www.genealogy.com/forum/surnames/topics/bacon/4017/ (Jonathan Bacon IV)

dealings too. In fact, what's reported is that he failed at farming, became a stage coach driver and eventually disappeared. One account of his disappearance says he died mysteriously while driving the stage coach, but another says he simply gave up and abandoned his family.[8] Whichever account is true, it's reported that the younger Jonathan's wife had to endure a difficult remaining life on her own.

The main point to be made from this early history is that there seems to have been a pattern of mediocrity that hindered this family from being successful. Other branches of the well-populated Bacon family tree scattered up and down the former eastern colonies seemed to be doing well and were particularly influential in developing the new country. But somehow that ability passed over the branch from Ward, Massachusetts.

And so, Sumner Bacon begins his life as the youngest sibling in a family that seems to have trouble succeeding and making ends meet financially, a condition that gravitates from father to first son and interferes in the plan that would have made young Sumner an attorney. Perhaps it's just a dream they never figure out how to pursue as they struggle year after year to make their farm productive. Decades later though, all of that comes to bear directly on the development of a man who would eventually help change the history of Texas.

Some Documentation Issues

When I started the research for this book, I found it frequently reported that Jonathan the father died some-where around 1809 and that Sumner left home in 1810 to

---

[8] Ibid (Notes for Jonathan Bacon V)

go out on his own. But that sequence didn't "feel" right somehow. So, a bit of further study did find the truth that both Jonathan the father and Jonathan the first son moved from Greenfield, Massachusetts to Oppenheim, New York in about 1820 where they again took up farming.[9] What I uncovered is that the father lived there a long time even applying for a soldier's pension at the age of seventy-three [10] because he'd served under General Washington in the Revolutionary War.[11] According to the DAR Magazine, Jonathan the father lived in Oppenheim until his death in July 1848 when he would have been almost 90 years old.[12]

Now I need to emphasize that I am first and foremost a minister and then a historian as a distant lower discipline. In other words, I'm motivated by ministry but interested in history, and I realize that some really serious historians have written that young Sumner left home AFTER his father Jonathan had died. A number of others have chosen to skip over this issue perhaps because they couldn't find the documentation. Nevertheless, I discovered two credible sources that have the father Jonathan living until July 1848 when he passed away in Oppenheim, New York. There's no report of an earlier death in the public records of either Ward or Greenfield, Massachusetts which was the motivation to keep searching until the trail leading to the family's final place of residence was eventually discovered.

In addition, it seems unlikely to me that young Sumner would leave his mother to fend for herself so soon after the

---

[9] Ibid
[10] Ibid
[11] Daughters of the American Revolution Magazine, Vol. XLVII, July 1915, p. 25
[12] Ibid

death of his father. There's evidence that Jonathan the older son was off on his own during those years in Dudley, Massachusetts where he eventually marries and joins the local militia (in 1813) during the War of 1812. Only after all that does he return to Greenfield to wind up purchasing his own small farm instead of joining with his mother. That seems to support the idea that the father was still living. Also, the daughter Betsy had married Anson Hitchcock in 1807 and had already departed from the Bacon farm to start her own family.[13]

Because of all that moving around and the fact that the documentation is inconsistent, it makes more sense to me that Sumner leaves home to seek his own life with his father still living and overseeing the family farm. What kind of future hero would have picked up everything and left his mother to fend for herself on a farm that had a history of difficulty? It doesn't seem to fit the Puritan values he would have received nor the basic character of a man who's willing to confront the extreme hardships of wilderness travel in the soon-coming search for his eventual destiny.

There's no evidence that Sumner stayed around past 1810 though, so it's agreed that he leaves the family somewhere around that time and goes out on his own most likely in response to a combination of several influences:

☐ Ongoing economic difficulty in his family
☐ Probable heir to the family farm at that time would have been the older son Jonathan

---

[13] http://www.genealogy.com/forum/surnames/topics/bacon/4017/ (Notes on Betsy)

☐ Population decrease in Greenfield between 1790 and 1810 to less than 1,000 people depresses the local economic environment[14]

☐ The religiosity of his church denomination which later documentation shows he disapproved of

☐ His desire to establish himself and make his own money

☐ The leading of the Holy Spirit toward his future destiny in the Texas territory

The Second Great Awakening

Another thing to keep in mind as young Sumner prepares to leave home is that the *Second Great Awakening* began about 1790, the very year he was born. And it lasts until about 1840 so that for most of his entire life, this significant move of God is in full force and responsible for pushing many people westward toward new lives and new fortunes in the frontier areas that are just starting to explode when he leaves his home in Greenfield.

As we go forward, keep in mind also that young Sumner was raised in a denomination (Congregational/Puritans) that had given energy to the *First Great Awakening* in the early 18th century in both positive and negative ways: positive in the sense that it was a dedicated bible-based denomination but negatively as well because its record of intolerance towards other Protestant denominations actually pushed believers toward those newly emerging alternatives. Going forward through the Revolutionary War and into the early 19th century, the Congregational Denomination fails to keep pace with the rate of new conversions and those other more recently established

---

[14] https://www.sec.state.ma.us/mhc/mhcpdf/townreports/CT-Valley/gre.pdf

denominations are more successful at achieving recognition in the new country of America where there's freedom of religion and the states can no longer favor and align themselves with particular church groups to the exclusion of other groups.

As the *Second Great Awakening* sweeps the country, there are revivals and camp meetings everywhere. Those revivals produce millions of new converts who become members in existing evangelical denominations (e.g. Baptists and Presbyterians) and even ignite the formation and expansion of new denominations (e.g. Methodists).[15] As young Sumner is leaving home no later than 1810 at the age of 20, he will be confronted with an environment of economic and geographic expansion, fortune seeking, opportunity, and evangelical explosion that will help shape a young man into an *unlikely* hero who will significantly influence the history of Texas. But that part comes a bit later!

---

[15] https://en.wikipedia.org/wiki/Second_Great_Awakening

But He knows the way I take; When He has tried me, I shall come forth as gold.

Job 23:10

TWO: IT'S A LONG WAY TO DAMASCUS

So, our unlikely future hero goes out on his own to seek a new life and perhaps as well the prominence that has eluded his family since before he was born. He will never return and he will never see his family again. That part of his story has been completed and although he doesn't know it yet, he has embarked on a special adventure, a plan that God has personally put together for His purposes and glory.

The main challenge for that plan at the start is that Sumner has few skills and apparently little education to build his future on. Years later we find commentaries to the fact that he lacked even a basic grasp of grammar and spelling.[16] So it seems that he'd managed to avoid any kind of formal education in his early years most probably devoting his energies to working on the family farm. Apparently, it needed all the help it could get.

In addition, his life experiences to this point have majored in mediocrity and under-achieving and they've become his reference point. One wonders if perhaps he couldn't have taken more notice of the accomplishments of some of the prominent members of the family church in Greenfield and reasoned that it might be possible for him to reach those higher things for himself. If so, it didn't show up for quite a while as we'll see further along in the story.

Now there are different accounts and time lines laid out by various historians for how young Sumner lives his next 15 years. So, the sequence and timing of events in this chapter are largely based from conclusions I had to make

---

[16] https://tshaonline.org/handbook/online/articles/fba03

from my study of the available documentation that was often inconsistent about the specifics. But there's enough good information available to provide a general direction and some reasonable assumptions about the timing of events in this key part of Sumner's life.

When he leaves home in 1810, he's either walking on foot or riding on horseback, maybe even riding in a basic wagon of some sort. He had used a buggy in the past but had managed to turn it over somehow in the weeks before he left home[17] so he most likely departs on horseback. He would have carried little money, enough food to get started on and the rest he makes for himself as he goes along. His general direction is south and west, certainly not in a straight line, as he goes from Greenfield, Massachusetts to western Pennsylvania and from there down the Ohio River Valley to the Mississippi River that he then follows south eventually winding up in Arkansas.

According to credible sources, that's a trip of more than 1,500 miles keeping in mind that in the early 19th century there are no highways, no direct routes from Point A to Point B, a few trading posts here and there and lots of inhospitable challenges to deal with including some difficult weather, rugged terrain and a host of some really ornery people. The young farm hand that starts out on such a trip will have to grow into a toughened *"man of the wilderness"* just to survive, which surely is what the Lord had in mind when they had departed...*together.*

Keep in mind also that when young Sumner leaves home, he's not yet a believer according to the biblical definition. True enough he'd attended the family church and they

---

[17] "Pistol Packing Preachers" by Barbara Barton, p. 25

were apparently active members of that church in Greenfield. But there's a difference between going to church and being a believer and by his own account later in life he doesn't become a believer until after he arrives in Arkansas and experiences his own personal self-confessed conversion. That means that for about 15 years of difficult travel and life on the frontier, he has to depend on himself to survive. He doesn't have a personal relationship with the Holy Spirit so he wouldn't have realized that by faith he could've counted on help to be available to get him through all the hardships he was facing on a daily basis. He's described as being *"unsociable, skeptical in his spiritual thoughts and critical of preachers and their teachings."*[18]

He usually feels lonely with a lot of time on his hands to think and wonder about life and where he's going to wind up. He worries sometimes about food and Indians and gun slingers and getting lost and the winter weather and a lot of things he wouldn't have fully considered before he left home. At first, he's homesick and wonders why he was so intent on leaving his family and going out on his own. He misses his parents and his brother and he doesn't know when or if he'll ever see them again. He occasionally questions whether or not he made the right decision. And once in a while he even thinks about going back to Greenfield, until he remembers the reasons why he left. He didn't just leave on a whim from one day to the next. He had thought about it, discussed it with his father and mother and they had decided together that what was best for their family was for him to leave home and seek his

---

[18] http://www.cleburnetimes review.com/news/lifestyles/mike-beard-sumner-bacon-s-mission-in-texas-endures/article_36fb33e0-489b-5a55-bd55-eeda64f816b4.html

own life. No one though, would have envisioned that he would wind up in a frontier location fifteen hundred miles to the southwest from the New England countryside they had always known and that it would take him more than fifteen years to find out where life (and God) would be taking him.

The truth is, not all that much is known about the details of his trip but most certainly he would have had to make use of the experience he had acquired as a farm worker and handyman. He works wherever he can find someone hiring especially at harvest time and he stays at particular locations until the work dries up and he has to move on, always to the south and west. He's accustomed to wearing buckskin britches and a hunting shirt and most certainly he fits well into the frontier environment he's traveling through.[19] Many nights he builds a camp fire and cooks whatever game he was able to trap or shoot that day. He sleeps there at night, lightly instinctively alert for encroachers, human and otherwise. Other nights it's raining and cold and those are miserable, uncomfortable times when Sumner thinks about having a stationary home, warm and cozy with a fire in the fireplace and protection from the elements.

To provide some additional context, young Sumner would have surely heard at some point that the U.S. had again become involved in a war with England. That war started in 1812 and ended in February of 1815, and most of the related action was happening back in the direction he'd come from. He's surely concerned about his family and we can only wonder if he ever knew that his brother Jonathan

---

[19] Ibid

had joined a militia in 1814.[20] Whatever his thoughts were, he didn't go back to find out. He's committed to a new life in pursuit of his destiny. The bridge that could take him back home has been burned.

At some point in his trip he hires onto a surveying party and follows along with them to wind up in Arkansas[21] in about 1822-23. His next "career move" is to join the US Army as a private which he *endures* for two years (1823-24) trying unsuccessfully to fit in. So, he opts out when his initial enlistment is completed. All the while his regiment is stationed in Fort Smith, Arkansas.[22]

In addition to what folks said about him before, now he's described as really gruff, rough and profane which some think is a rub off from this short stay in the Army. He sure didn't learn all that back on the family farm in Massachusetts but itinerate travelling and a couple of years in the U.S. Army have changed a lot of people, on the one hand helping to develop confidence and determination and submission to authority even while on the other negatively impacting their demeanor and ways of speaking. The maturing Sumner has some things coming in his future that will require a man that's rough and ready, unafraid of the elements, confident in his ability to endure and survive, determined to pursue and finish what he sets out to do. Those other, negative things the Holy Spirit will have to take care of in His special way.

After his discharge from the Army, his next move is to go to work again as a hired hand, this time for a family there

---

[20] http://www.genealogy.com/forum/surnames/topics/bacon/4017/ (See notes on Jonathan IV to find the information on Jonathan V)
[21] https://tshaonline.org/handbook/online/articles/fba03
[22] http://www.cumberland.org/hfpc/minister/BaconS.htm

in Arkansas. Keep in mind he had left home fourteen years before in 1810 so by now he's surely wondering if he's ever going to find something in life that's meaningful, rewarding and more permanent, that actually accomplishes something. He's met a lot of people on his way down to Arkansas but he didn't stay with them very long: no business ventures that survived, no farms owned, no marriage, no family, nothing of real value has stuck to Sumner Bacon yet. In his present appearance and appraisal, and back in his buckskins again, he's not looked at as anyone of substance or talent or ability or future, or as anyone of promise. He's an under-educated, profane man of the wilderness dressed in frontier garb who knows his way around a farm, a day laborer good with his hands but lacking in intellect.[23]

Arkansas had become an official U.S. Territory in 1819 and was still just a wilderness itself. An even wilder wilderness was in the vast area just to the west that the Mexicans called TEJAS and until recently it hadn't looked all that inviting because the only people that lived over there had been mostly a bunch of hostile Indians and some Catholic priests. But Anglo-American settlers had finally started moving into TEJAS a few years ago even though according to what he'd been told, everybody had to become Catholic when they got there and learn to speak some Spanish. Those things didn't seem to be stopping anybody once they set their minds to it. So now in 1826 almost two years out of the Army, he naturally wants to know more about what TEJAS has to offer.

Things were indeed changing because the word had been out since 1821 that there was a really attractive land grant

---

[23] Ibid

program over there where folks could go and start over. Sumner had noticed some wagon trains coming through Arkansas on their way to TEJAS. Many of those folks were fleeing creditors back where he'd traveled through in the Ohio and Mississippi River Valleys including in particular some of the southern states like Tennessee, Ohio, Missouri, Mississippi and Alabama where economies had collapsed after the War of 1812.

Perhaps he thinks about trying to save enough money to join a wagon train and go over to TEJAS to buy some land and get established. He's seen posters everywhere saying the best way to take advantage of the land grant program and not get cheated is to connect with one of the authorized land grant organizers like the man so many folks are talking about by the name of Stephen F. Austin. Meanwhile, he's working as a farm laborer for the family there in Arkansas thinking about these things and hoping for something meaningful to happen in his life. He's got a little money saved up but what would he do over there? And where would he go? Was he really ready to settle down in one place and stop all his traveling?

Arriving in Damascus

In case you haven't quite gotten to the part in your Bible where the Apostle Paul meets Jesus on the Road to Damascus, you'll find an account of it in the Book of Acts, Chapter 9, verses 3 through 19. A similar thing is about to happen to our friend from Greenfield, Massachusetts but this time Damascus is in Arkansas.

Hopefully you remember from earlier that the *Second Great Awakening* is going on all over the country during most of the time of this story. Evangelists were hosting camp meetings even in the wilderness territories wherever a crowd of people could be assembled wanting to hear the Good News (Gospel) of Jesus Christ. It seems that folks were hungry for God in those days because putting together a group to hear the Word was easy.

Well, it turns out that in 1826 our now 36-year old friend, Sumner decides that it's time for him to attend one of those camp meetings even though according to observers of the day he's skeptical about church things and doesn't trust preachers. He probably had become curious wondering why so many people were going to those events. Certainly, he's talked to some of the folks after they'd been changed by those meetings and what they were describing to him was really different than what he'd experienced personally at the *Congregational* church back home. The one he chooses to finally go to is a Presbyterian camp meeting there in Arkansas and it winds up changing his life in the same way the Apostle Paul was changed all those years ago outside Damascus. The similarity is notable!

Now to help set the stage for what's about to happen, there were three major church denominations that had quite an impact on the American frontier including the area where Sumner had chosen to live these past few years: Presbyterians, Baptists and Methodists. Two of the three (Presbyterians and Baptists) were the main denominations that had received all the new converts during the *First Great Awakening* in the 18th century and they were again now in the following century at the forefront of the *Second Great Awakening.*

All three of these Protestant denominations had splintered off from the *Church of England* as reform groups and then found their way to the U.S. brought here by charismatic English leader-preachers. The earliest of the three to arrive in America was the *Baptist* denomination in 1638.[24] They eventually drew members from the *Puritans* who at the same time were dealing with lost membership to the Quakers and not taking kindly at all to either of these "competing" evangelical groups. The *Baptists* were followed by the *Presbyterians* who established their first Presbytery in Philadelphia in 1706. The *Methodists* missed the *First Great Awakening* in America but established their denomination here in 1784 just in time for the *Second Great Awakening*.

It seems that all Protestant denominations have to go through one or more membership splits sometime in their history and that occurred with the Presbyterians in 1810[25] which is *"coincidentally"* the year that Sumner de-parted from Greenfield, Massachusetts. The name of the group that split off was the *Cumberland Presbyterians* and the reason they went on their own was because they wanted to send quickly-prepared ministers out into the exciting turmoil of the *Second Great Awakening*. But the original denomination wanted their clergy to continue going through their full regimen of seminary education that required several years of study.

On a particular night in 1826 down in Arkansas, Sumner Bacon makes his way to a Cumberland Presbyterian camp meeting[26] perhaps encouraged by the people he works for or by other acquaintances in the area. He isn't a very sociable person, gruff and not so friendly but somebody had gotten through to him. Keep in mind that millions of Americans will have gone through a similar experience by the end of this great national move of God.

---

[24] https://en.wikipedia.org/wiki/Baptists
[25] https://en.wikipedia.org/wiki/Cumberland_Presbyterian_Church
[26] http://www.cumberland.org/hfpc/minister/BaconS.htm

Sumner Bacon has lived a hard life since he left home sixteen years ago. Nothing has improved in his life since he left. He's a day laborer and wonders sometimes what it might have been like to have become an attorney like his family originally planned. Perhaps he's a little depressed over his lack of accomplishment: no career, no money and no family. Yes, it's true he's under-educated but he's not stupid as later events will prove. He knows deep down inside he's capable of greater works than he's done so far and that he has a special destiny. He just hasn't been able to figure out yet what it is even though he's thought about it a lot.

So, he goes to a Cumberland Presbyterian revival meeting that night with a lot on his mind, with a lot of questions, hoping to hear something special, to get some answers for where his difficult, unrewarding life is going to go next. Or is he just stuck here in Arkansas at the end of a really long and difficult trail? What about TEJAS?

He listens carefully to the message the evangelist is preaching. He remembers hearing some of it years before back in the family church. The evangelist is a gifted speaker whose words gradually overcome the skepticism that Sumner had walked into the meeting with that night. There are questions he'd had about God that are finally being answered. For the first time in his life Sumner is coming to a real encounter with the Creator God of the Universe and he *really* likes what he's hearing.

He likes it so much that when the Evangelist completes his message and invites his audience to step forward to make a public profession of faith, Sumner Bacon comes out of his seat and before realizing what he's doing, before he can reason why he shouldn't be doing it, he comes up to the Evangelist and in an instant is converted from lost to found, from sinner to righteous, from darkness to light, from child of the devil to child of God. In an instant Sumner Bacon becomes a new creature[27] with a new life that carries with it a particular calling that he could not have known about before this special moment on a night down in Arkansas as one long, empty journey ends there in Damascus and a bright new one dawns leading to a new place and a new destiny. As he walks away that night, he's aware of a profound change.

---

[27] Holy Bible, 2 Corinthians 5:17

The gifts and the calling of God are irrevocable.

Romans 11:29

THREE: INTRODUCTION TO THE NEW ASSIGNMENT

It doesn't take Sumner very long to figure out that God has had a call on his life all along and that he's taken a really long time getting to that camp meeting down in Arkansas. It's suddenly clear to him that he's supposed to go into the ministry and start evangelizing that ever-growing group of doubters, non-believers and back-sliders there on the frontier that he'd just had the blessing of coming out from. He's 36 years old and his life is starting over. Now with his conversion comes a sense of urgency he'd not had before to pursue a calling he'd not been aware of before with a new set of priorities he'd never experienced before. True to the call of the Evangelist, he's literally *compelled* supernaturally to share with other folks what he's recently learned about God so they can know and experience the same sense of fulfillment he's now feeling.

From years of hardship on the trail, there's no fear in Sumner Bacon as he prepares for his new life. He'll share his testimony with anyone at any time and he's not shy about initiating the conversation. There's a special boldness he demonstrates and a determination to get started with his new life. Within a short time after his conversion, he comes to the conclusion that his destiny is in TEJAS but when any believer tries to pursue a calling, you can be sure there will be some formidable obstacles blocking the way that have to be dealt with before the process can get some traction. Sometimes the obstacles are real and other times they are deceptions that have no real power because they have come from the Adversary who has an interest in seeing to it that Christians never get started in the pursuit of their callings. There's probably nothing so frustrating for the Devil as Christians who're in pursuit of their God-given callings and know who they are in Christ.

The first obstacle is the fact that in 1826, it's absolutely illegal for anyone in Texas to hear preaching about the Protestant version of the Gospel. Up until 1821 while TEJAS belonged to Spain, the official mandated religion had been Catholicism but it wasn't strictly enforced. So, Protestant ministers had started coming into Texas in 1815 from that new Methodist denomination and the Baptists came close behind in 1820. They held some bible studies mostly in private residences and ministered to what was up to then a fairly sparse settler population scattered across a huge Territory.[28]

But in 1820, Spain introduced a land grant program to motivate an increased flow of Anglo settlers into TEJAS from the north. Just a year later Mexico won its independence from Spain and essentially continued the same land grant program. As soon as they could though, Mexico developed a new Constitution that was officially adopted in 1824 about the time Sumner was finishing up his stint in the Army. It was that new Constitution that had the big changes for religious Protestant settlers: each immigrant coming into the Territory would now be required by law to profess Catholic Christianity as their religion and only Catholic Priests would be allowed to perform ministry throughout the territory.[29] In addition, the teaching of the Word by anybody anywhere in the

---

[28] The Influence of Christianity on Early Texas History, p. 47
[29] Ibid, p. 48

territory would have to conform to Roman Catholic teaching guidelines.

The fact that his preaching will be illegal is of little relevance or concern to Sumner. Those kinds of details are simply inconveniences and there's not going to be anything that's big enough or important enough to impede a tough and determined, trail-tested Christian wilderness-man who traveled almost two thousand miles to find out what his calling is. *Obstacle #1 overcome!*

Before going any farther though, let me make it clear that while I am indeed a Protestant minister, I'm not prejudiced against any Christian faith group and I am not anti-Catholic by any means. Nevertheless, this was a time in Texas history when one important branch of Christianity became heavy-handed which staunch, free-minded folks are always going to resist. The fact is, religion became a major factor in the groundswell for independence and its impact has been largely overlooked by secular historians.

Now there is also a second hurdle for Sumner to consider: most of the Texas Territory in late 1826 is still unclaimed and very untamed. That means it's a very dangerous place to hang out because it's full of desperados, hostile Indians, Mexican soldiers looking for Protestant sympathizers to arrest and an opposing group of apathy-minded, anti-Protestant Anglo settlers. That includes Stephen F. Austin himself and none of them want Protestant evangelicals stirring up unrest and civil disobedience for the Mexican authorities to have to deal with. In June of 1825 Austin had signed his famous contract with the Mexican authorities to bring colonists into TEJAS and he wants no problems with those authorities that might cause them to change or cancel those arrangements.[30]

Local associates warn Sumner about the dangers, the Presbyterian leaderships in both Arkansas and Louisiana warn him about the dangers; but he doesn't give their good intentions any serious thought. He's already determined that his future is in what the new settlers are calling *"Texas"* and he's already decided to go there. Almost daily he sees hopeful settlers passing through, taking their families into those same dangers and he knows God is sending him to provide the spiritual connection they will need to be successful. If they can face the dangers there, so will he. *Obstacle #2 overcome!*

But there's a remaining detail that our friend must deal with: he's now a member of the Presbyterian denomination and he wants to go to *Texas* under their covering as an ordained minister. But even the Cumberland folks with their relaxed requirements for sending out less experienced ministers don't think Sumner is ready to go share the Gospel he's just started learning about without some instruction and preparation, especially since he's determined to go into such a dangerous area. This will prove to be his biggest obstacle as he starts trying to put together his first trip into *Texas*.

On two separate occasions starting in early 1827, Sumner Bacon officially proposes his candidacy for the ministry to the Presbyterian leadership and is denied.[31] According to several credible historians, the Cumberland Presbytery

---

[30] Ibid, p. 52

[31] http://www.cleburnetimes review.com/news/lifestyles/mike-beard-sumner-bacon-s-mission-in-texas-endures/article_36fb33e0-489b-5a55-bd55-eeda64f816b4.html

thought that in addition to being a novice, he had an insufficient grasp of basic grammar and spelling that he should work on before they could agree to release him to go in their name into his proposed ministry. They estimated it would take up to two years for him to grow enough to meet their basic requirements for at least a license if not outright ordination.

In between the two denials Sumner makes a tacit effort to work on his educational shortcomings. But, at 37 years of age and with little academic experience in his past, he doesn't get very far with all the *"book-learning"* they want and grows ever more impatient to begin the pursuit of his new calling.

While he's waiting though, he doesn't let any grass grow under his determination and commitment as he waits for the Presbytery to come into agreement with him. So, he starts to minister on his own locally there in Arkansas organizing a few meetings here and there, getting some ministry experience under his belt while he's also trying to learn how to spell and speak better. Those early efforts in the ministry weren't all that great according to the local minister-leaders who observed his work and their rather cryptic evaluation was that he was a bit too *erratic*.[32] For a new minister who had just recently converted and was relying largely on Word knowledge he'd heard in his family church almost 20 years before, "erratic" was probably a generous grade: "E" for erratic.

Finally, the day came to make the second application for licensing. And, it was soon followed by the second denial on the grounds that their student hadn't applied himself

---

[32] http://www.cumberland.org/hfpc/minister/BaconS.htm

enough to the education his leaders thought was so necessary. That was the tipping point for Sumner who had enough ministry experience under his belt by this time to feel confident for a future success in Texas. It never did take all that much anyway to make the wilderness man from Massachusetts feel confident.

And so, unable to contain himself any longer, Sumner Bacon sets out in 1828 on his own as an unlicensed, "unauthorized" lay minister dressed in his buckskin britches and hunting shirt and armed with his six gun and some bibles he's purchased with his own money.[33] His destination on this first trip is east Texas and the future official History of the Cumberland Presbyterian Denomination will say that Sumner Bacon was *the first independent lay evangelist to preach on Texas soil.*[34]

By this point in the story, if I've told it well enough, you should be convinced that the Rev. Sumner Bacon is a serious, determined, passionate, tough, persistent, committed, Christian-wilderness-man and that just about anything is going to be possible in his future, especially now that God is helping him.

Obstacle #3 overcome! And as the rest of his story unfolds, don't be surprised at what he still has in front of him in his extraordinary life.

---

[33] Ibid + https://tshaonline.org/handbook/online/articles/fba03

[34] http://www.cleburnetimes review.com/news/lifestyles/mike-beard-sumner-bacon-s-mission-in-texas-endures/article_36fb33e0-489b-5a55-bd55-eeda64f816b4.html

I can do all things through Christ the anointed One, who strengthens me.

Philippians 4:13

FOUR: MAKING UP FOR LOST TIME
(1828-1835)

To say that Sumner Bacon hit the ground running once he decided to go out to Texas on his own would be an understatement. He'd waited perhaps 18 months or more after his conversion trying to go through channels and meet the minimum requirements of his Cumberland leadership. But, there just didn't seem to be a way to get to an acceptable arrangement. We know from documentation of his later life that it was really important to him to go out to Texas with Presbyterian credentials. But eventually he feels compelled to go on and answer his call. He prays about it as he'd been taught by his church group in Arkansas and then makes the decision to proceed on his own without his Denomination's authorization. So, as we now know he purchases supplies and some bibles and off he goes into the dangerous Texas Territory on his own.

Some historians say he left Arkansas as late as the fall of 1829[35] but I've chosen a slightly earlier time line for this story because it seems to fit better with what comes later. Also, many of the other historians seemed to prefer it as well which is reassuring but not the main reason for choosing it. So, in 1828 as Sumner is departing for Texas, the Mexican land grant program has been in effect for about seven years motivating thousands of new mostly Protestant Anglo settlers to come into the Territory. At the same time the Mexican Constitution in its fourth year

---

[35] https://tshaonline.org/handbook/online/articles/fba03 + ALSO: *Voice in the Wilderness: A History of the Cumberland Presbyterian Church in Texas* by Robert D. Brackenridge

bans the preaching of Protestant Christianity to those same new settlers.

Some Key Issues to Understand about Christianity

There are a couple of things that need to be especially emphasized in the early part of this chapter because of how some of our secular historians mischaracterize the religious situation that lay-minister Sumner Bacon is getting himself involved in. The first is the generalization that most of the incoming settlers weren't Christian-believing church folks. In my view that's a false conclusion and ignores that the influx of settlers from the Ohio and Mississippi River Valleys were coming out of perhaps the greatest Spiritual Awakening in the history of the country where millions of people were converted just like had happened to Sumner. To be sure there were a lot of those settlers who weren't yet converted but the ratio of true Christians among the total group of settlers was way higher than what's usually portrayed.

The fact is, this particular mischaracterization is based on the observation that the new settlers coming in weren't committed church-goers as if that's the principal determinant for whether or not they were believers or unbelievers. Could it have been though, that the reason they didn't attend church so regularly was that there were NO Protestant churches to go to except a few illegal, clandestine house groups where everybody could have been arrested in the middle of Sunday morning worship? Could it also perhaps have been that the only churches authorized in the entire territory were of the Catholic Denomination and that their services were really different than the new settlers were used to and were conducted in the Spanish language? And could it have also been that throughout these years there was a chronic shortage of priests that were available to tend to the people's spiritual needs? Even to attend a Catholic gathering required traveling long distances through the hazards and dangers that were part of the regular landscape of that day. Given all of that, I probably wouldn't have been a regular church-goer either, even as the Bible Thumper I would surely have become anyway!

A second mischaracterization says that most of the Protestant ministers coming illegally into the territory were charlatans and deceivers who were after the settlers' money. To start with, the settlers didn't have very much money which is why they were coming into such a dangerous place to start over. Indeed, many were coming to escape their creditors and have a chance at a new life. And only God knows how many of the folks who started their long journeys out to Texas lost whatever money they had scraped together to desperados and disasters and cheaters before they could reach their destination.

Also, the secular thinking about these things reveals a profound lack of understanding of the callings that motivate ministers and of the supernatural spiritual power that fueled the *Second Great Awakening*. Most of those Protestant ministers wanting to go into Texas in 1828 were called by God to go there and they brought with them the energy and revelation that were such a vital part of the Protestant movement of those days. The fact is, most of those ministers were being PUSHED into Texas by God Himself so that the power of His Word could be released there to form a Protestant foundation for the development of a territory that a mere seventeen years later in 1845 would become the 28th state in the Union.

Sumner Bacon was called by God to go into Texas and he had waited a long time to go there. He wasn't a charlatan, he didn't know enough to be one, and he wasn't after the Settlers' money. He went there pushed by God to collect souls for the Kingdom of God and to communicate the Word of God to people who needed to hear it and needed to hear it in the English language. One thing that secular historians can't be expected to understand is the deep-seated drive that true believers possess to HEAR the Word preached on a regular basis by skilled and knowledgeable preachers because it acts supernaturally to strengthen our faith for dealing successfully with adversity and fear and the inevitable disappointments of life.

On the Road Again

So, Sumner Bacon is now off to Texas on his own and it's 1828. He enters through Nacogdoches County and eventually penetrates the Territory as far as the town of San Felipe,[36] the cultural center of the first Stephen F. Austin colony located about 45 miles west of the future city of Houston.[37] It doesn't take him very long to start distributing bibles and wining souls for the Kingdom of God. A truly called evangelist equipped by the Holy Spirit can be quite effective with just a basic knowledge of the Bible. What they lack in academic study and preparation can be largely compensated for with passion, energy and the speaking ability to connect with an audience in a way that key points are easily understood. Sometimes preachers can get a little too "eloquent" and speak over the heads of their audiences, but it's doubtful such a thing ever happened with Sumner Bacon in the Pulpit.

---

[36] https://tshaonline.org/handbook/online/articles/fba03
[37] https://en.wikipedia.org/wiki/San_Felipe,_Texas

According to historians the man who had been difficult to communicate with in the past becomes a super-communicator under the mantle of God's calling, and stories about his ministry soon begin to accumulate to the surprise of his Cumberland friends and associates back in Arkansas.

Fortunately for history, the documentation for Sumner's remaining life is somewhat more complete than for the years leading up to his ministry and it tells a really special story. The way I see it, that remaining story needs to be told in three separate parts:

☐ The first is the seven-year period from his entry into Texas in 1828 until the latter part of 1835 when the struggle for Texas Independence calls him away from the ministry for a brief time.

☐ The second part covers the period from late in 1835 until well into 1836 when Sumner becomes actively and directly involved in the war-effort for Texas independence.

☐ And the final segment covers the remaining eight years of his life from late 1836 to 1844 when finally, he becomes an influential Christian leader and *bona fide* hero in the new Republic of Texas.

This chapter then deals with the first of the three periods and the first exciting years of Sumner Bacon's ministry.

The Early Years of Ministry

The moment Sumner gets into Nacogdoches County, he starts distributing bibles and talking about Jesus. He soon establishes a headquarters in the nearby town of San

Augustine[38] and nothing is going to stop him from doing God's work. But he's not naive and since the Mexican authorities are enforcing the legal status of Catholicism as the only allowed religion across the territory, Sumner does his preaching on the move. He preaches for a while in a particular place and when government pursuit seems imminent, he moves on to a new place.[39] He manages to stay a few steps ahead of the *Federales* and before very long he's out of bibles and there are a bunch of new Christians there in East Texas.

Historians agree that in 1830, after two years of staying just ahead of those *"Mexican Protestant Police"* and being constantly on the move, Sumner writes to Stephen F. Austin to apply for the position of Chaplain for the colony that Austin is raising up by the land grant deal he had negotiated in 1825. It's said that the answer written back to Sumner was polite but nonetheless a clear and blunt denial letter.

As I thought more about this little factoid of Texas history, it occurred to me that Sumner is probably thinking about the possibility of a safer lifestyle and line of work than he had experienced so far. Perhaps he doesn't realize that at the time Austin is politically opposed to Protestant preaching and that he's looking at it as a threat to his colonization business. For that reason alone, even if Austin was unaware of Sumner's growing reputation as an evangelist, he would have denied any Protestant candidate for such a sensitive position.

On Sumner's part, he wouldn't have fully understood how a professing Christian would allow such unbiblical

---

[38] http://www.texashighways.com/eat/item/6194-bacon-146-s-bibles
[39] https://tshaonline.org/handbook/online/articles/fba03

reasoning to block the furtherance of God's work in developing the Texas Territory. Thus, Austin's denial letter would have been unexpected representing a confirmation for Sumner that the religious/political debate that had increasingly raged in Texas since 1825 had become more confrontational than he'd thought.

The fact is, most secular historians either overlook this debate or don't do it justice so I want to make clear that all Protestant ministers of that day in Texas were not only dodging the Mexican *Federales* but also a VERY hostile "loyalist" Anglo segment that did not want these preachers coming into their areas. They saw them as a threat to the peaceful pursuit of their new lives in a frontier area that was already dangerous enough without stirring up problems with the Mexican authorities. Some in that anti-preacher group were Protestant Christian believers but they were putting their personal interests ahead of the interests of the Kingdom of God.

Their resistance against the preachers wasn't mild or just a topic of polite debate. In fact, more often than not the Anglo opposition was more of a threat than the Mexican authorities. Many an innocent assembling of believers around the Territory in the late 1820's and early 30's were broken up by local Anglo loyalists where injury was inflicted on the offending ministers unless pro-Protestant defenders showed up to protect the innocent "law-breakers." So, it was necessary for evangelists, Sumner included, to arrange for security at many of their events.

Now it didn't take very long for Sumner Bacon to start developing quite a reputation for dealing with all the threats that came against his ministry. Many a story came out of the Territory and began to make their way back to

Arkansas and beyond about the latest scrape that Rev. Bacon had faced and somehow gotten out of. Those stories are a fascinating insight into a unique ministry and you will find several of the most famous "legends" assembled together in the next chapter.

Fortunately for history, as the years go by it becomes increasingly clear to most of those problematic Anglo settlers that having religious freedom would be way preferable to a government-mandated religion they're not familiar with. Gradually the pro-Protestant group grows and increases in influence and without that happening, there might never have developed the move of civil resistance that eventually produces the Republic of Texas. Even Stephen F. Austin eventually changes his stance and if he hadn't, it's doubtful that today we would all be calling him the *Father of Texas*.

Back for More Bibles

In late 1832, after four years in the Texas wilds and leaving an untold but impressive number of new Christian converts in his wake, Sumner decides he needs more bibles and goes back to Arkansas for supplies. Once again, he applies to the Arkansas Presbytery for his Ministry License and is again denied.[40] The denial for Sumner is of course an *"incidental detail"* that doesn't interfere with his plan to get possession of the largest possible number of bibles both in English and Spanish to take back to Texas. He'll either go back as a credentialed Presbyterian minister or an unauthorized independent lay minister, but either way he's going back to Texas to finish the job God has

---

[40] http://www.cumberland.org/hfpc/minister/BaconS.htm

called him to do. And, he's going back there with a whole bunch of bibles as well, one way or another.

In the search for those bibles, God provides an interesting and impactful source of supply. In early 1833 Sumner meets with Rev. Benjamin Chase, a Presbyterian minister and an agent for the *American Bible Society* who at first warns Sumner not to go back to Texas because of the danger. Some historians believe the two men had previously met perhaps in Tennessee when Sumner had originally traveled through there.[41] Seeing his friend's determination to return to Texas, Chase personally recommends Sumner to the *Society* and it agrees to commission him as its first regular agent in Texas.[42] Suddenly Sumner has access to all the bibles he can carry but decides for his own reasons not to accept the salary that's made available to him in the new position.[43]

And so, Sumner prepares to go back to Texas to resume his itinerate ministry even though he faces threats against his life and constant pressure from those fore-mentioned groups that don't want him there. Once again, he has no credentials and comes totally on his own. But this time he comes with a lot of bibles probably in a wagon because he has such a large load on his hands. Historians say that in the two-year period from 1833 to 1835, the Rev. Sumner Bacon personally distributes more than 2,000 *Society* bibles against almost unbelievable odds. It's worth mentioning here that in order to have gotten possession of

---

[41] Pistol Packing Preachers" by Barbara Barton, p. 21

[42] Ibid

[43] http://www.cleburnetimes review.com/news/lifestyles/mike-beard-sumner-bacon-s-mission-in-texas-endures/article_36fb33e0-489b-5a55-bd55-eeda64f816b4.html

that many bibles, Sumner would have had to travel to the nearest warehouse operated by the *Bible Society* which happened in those days to be in Nashville, Tennessee.[44] And for future reference, the Headquarters of the *Cumberland Presbyterians* was in Burns, Tennessee which is not far from Nashville.

Later it will be said by *Cumberland* leaders that *"he scattered the Word of Life from San Antonio to the Sabine with an industrious hand."* Keep in mind that it was still illegal to be distributing bibles in Texas but Sumner Bacon took no heed of that and put bibles in the hands of anybody who wanted one, both English and Spanish.

Of course, that isn't all that Sumner did from 1833 to 1835 because he also continues to organize those camp meetings of his and preach the Word of God wherever he can get a crowd together. Some of the legends about his ministry come out of this period as the Territory is approaching the tipping point for dealing with the issue of its two *"religions."* People try to stop him and other people try to injure him and still others try to kill him, but nothing can cut this man off from his calling. He escapes, he overcomes and he succeeds. And in that really special process, a lot of people in Texas are converted to Protestant Christianity.

In March of 1835 after distributing all those bibles and leading thousands of settlers over some seven years to their eternities with Christ, Rev. Sumner Bacon again goes back to present himself for ordination but this time he goes to the newly established Louisiana Presbytery. With the help of his *Bible Society* friend Rev. Ben Chase and his

---

[44] "The Centennial History of the American Bible Society," The Macmillan Company, 1916, p. 175

own now-persuasive speaking ability, Bacon is FINALLY licensed and ordained a Cumberland Presbyterian Minister.[45]

Of course, in typical Sumner-fashion, the ordination ceremony has to be shortened from the normal two days to only one so that Sumner can get on with his preparations for joining the struggle for Texas independence.[46] But the Louisiana Presbytery realizes they're dealing with an extraordinary man of God and so they agree to an extraordinary validation. They suspend all the usual educational requirements making sure to call their decision *"an extraordinary case and by no means a precedent for future actions."*[47] Later, *Cumberland* church leaders will write that even though Sumner's *"literary attainments"* hadn't reached their standards, his great usefulness in the field more than warranted this unusual exception to their requirements for ordination.[48]

Sumner doesn't care what their file notes say about him, he's finally ordained after nine years (1826-1835) of waiting and hoping. He has credentials now, he's a licensed Presbyterian Evangelist authorized by his Denomination to carry out his work in their name, under their covering wherever God sends him. It's a big day for Rev. Sumner Bacon and he thinks back to those frustrating years in the wilderness on his way to Arkansas when he was wondering what his life would be like and whether or not he'd ever amount to anything.

---

[45] https://tshaonline.org/handbook/online/articles/fba03
[46] http://www.cleburnetimes review.com/news/lifestyles/mike-beard-sumner-bacon-s-mission-in-texas-endures/article_36fb33e0-489b-5a55-bd55-eeda64f816b4.html
[47] Ibid
[48] http://www.cumberland.org/hfpc/minister/BaconS.htm

He may have thought about sending a letter to his family back in Massachusetts but there's no record he ever did that. By this time, he's been gone twenty-five years and he's not sure where they might be living. According to the research they're living in Oppenheim, New York which Sumner probably didn't know about. Anyway, it's not easy to get overland mail from the southwestern frontier all the way back two thousand miles to where he came from in Massachusetts. If there ever were any letters among the family, they've been lost to history.

What a change this man has undergone since he decided to become friends with Jesus. But there's more to come because Sumner Bacon is far from finished...*by a long shot!* In fact, he's just getting started!

With God all things are possible.

Matthew 19:26

FIVE: HOW SUMNER BACON BECOMES LEGENDARY

One of the characteristics of the Rev. Bacon all of his days was that he was really tough and *scrappy*. He faced challenges and problems constantly but confronted them head on and wouldn't allow anything to interfere with what he had to do. He was determined to carry out his calling and whatever got in his way was ignored, circumvented or run over. Because of all that *scrappiness* and the favor of God working right there through him, stories began to emerge about how Sumner had repeatedly walked away from impossible situations without having to use his six-gun. To be sure, he always had that pistol of his at the ready but there are no stories about how he got out of trouble by shooting folks or even threatening to shoot. He just seemed to rely on his new-found ability to talk his way out of almost anything with the help certainly of the Holy Spirit.

A number of these stories have been written down and it wouldn't be fair to let you go away without knowing about them. There are too many to put into this story so I've selected a few favorites. Most of these events happened during the ministry years covered in the previous chapter and are fondly remembered all through the writings of Texas historians. There's no other figure from those early circuit-riding days that comes close to Sumner Bacon either in the number of stories that are told or in the reverence that people have for them just because of how special they are. Special stories about a special man of God become legends in the history of Texas!

Legend No. 1:

One day as Sumner Bacon was traveling alone in East Texas, a couple of rough characters attacked him, knocked him off his horse and proceeded to work him over with their fists. It became obvious to Sumner that they wanted him dead and they wanted his horses. But he hesitated to pull his six-shooter because as a minister he preferred to try talking about the situation to see if that would work instead of having to shoot folks. It didn't look good for ministers to be shooting people before they got a fair chance to meet up with Jesus.

So, Sumner got an idea *"from some place"* that he should ask these men if he could pray for them before they finished killing him. The two men thought it was such a unique request, they gave their permission. So, he prayed a powerful Sumner prayer and called on the Almighty to make things right for everybody. When he'd finished praying, both of those young ruffians repented and became his good friends.

Now it seems that these new acquaintances of Sumner's were originally the most notorious horse thieves in the area and part of a horse-thieving family. When the boys came home that day, their hard-hearted mother asked about their activities and when told that they hadn't killed the preacher when they had the chance, she wanted to know why. Her boys were quick to reply with this explanation: *"We never saw such a man. We would as soon kill our own father as him."* There's no record of what their mama said next but it surely must have occurred to her that their horse-stealing business might soon be coming to an end.

Legend No. 2:

One day in that same region of East Texas the Rev. Bacon was preaching to an outdoor audience, which was a pretty common occurrence in those days, about the plan of salvation. Suddenly his preaching was interrupted by some approaching cowboys who were making a lot of noise to disrupt one of those illegal meetings they didn't think should be happening. These men had the same idea as the two previous characters which was that the parson needed killing. But just about the time Sumner started thinking he was going to go and be with Jesus, up rode his two new friends, the now unemployed horse thieves. As former outlaws they were a lot more intimidating than the cowboys had wanted to reckon with so the cowboys quickly agreed to back off from the lynching they had planned for Rev. Bacon and went quickly on their way.

Legend No. 3:

One day in the spring of 1832, the Revs. Bacon and Needham J. Alford planned a revival near the present-day town of Milam. As they spread the word about it, some folks could hardly wait to attend while others were sorely aggravated about it. That's just the way Texas was in those days and everybody knew that at every meeting a ruckus could break out and often did.

Among those who didn't want the meeting in their town was a tough hombre named John Gaines who owned the Sabine River Ferry. He was influential in the area because his ferryboat was important to travelers and to the folks who lived nearby. He thought the planned revival would be an overt act that defied the local rules and that it should therefore be stopped, end of story. So, he gathered several like-minded men to help take care of the two preachers when they eventually showed up.

One of the men who joined him was a known local troublemaker named Johnson who said he would whip the first preacher to try to stand behind the make-shift pulpit that had been provided that day for the revival. And he was carrying a really angry looking bullwhip that made his intentions all too clear.

The two ministers arrived about that time just as a riot was about to break out between all the folks who DID want to hear the preaching pitted against Gaines, Johnson and the men who DIDN'T want to hear a word of it. But as the two preachers walked up, the trouble makers begin to re-evaluate their situation because Rev. Alford was a big, robust, muscular man who had no fear of the hecklers and the other preacher named Sumner Bacon was to their surprise packing a big six-gun in plain sight. They didn't have to resort to violence though because Rev. Alford steps forward and says directly to the local bullies: *"I am able to take a whipping as any man on this ground"* and the opposition quickly and quietly retired to a safer area as the revival started with Alford taking the pulpit first. As the legend goes, Johnson the trouble maker with the bullwhip left the revival and mysteriously died that night. No one ever knew why he died but there was a popularly circulated suspicion that somehow there had been some divine intervention involved. It's probably no surprise that they didn't have any more trouble from that group of men for the rest of the revival which lasted several more days.

Legend No. 4:

Nevertheless, as the revival continues, it becomes Sumner's turn to share the Word and he starts to speak to the people in his usual simple but passionate delivery that so effectively connected folks to the Word. But before very long, trouble tries to enter upon the scene again but from a different direction this time as the local *alcalde* (mayor) sends word for Rev. Bacon to stop preaching. The news quickly spreads all over the area about all the trouble these preachers are having keeping this revival going which so many had wanted and looked forward to. Before very long, an extra-large crowd of folks gathers to hear Sumner's preaching and all of his special friends in the area are standing all around the meeting area armed and daring anyone to try to hurt or stop *"God's special messenger."* The sermon is then delivered without further incident and apparently the mayor got busy with some other local matters and "forgot" about the *"cease and desist order"* he'd sent over a bit earlier.

Legend No. 5:

On one particular occasion Sumner was arrested in Nacogdoches for handing out Bibles and was put in the local jail house. Folks figured he would be there for a spell because distributing bibles was strictly against the federal law and had become a serious offense especially in the opinion of the local Catholic Church. But somehow the Rev. Bacon was able to arrange for his release really quickly and out he came a few minutes later smiling and ready to get a group together to go face the next challenge.

That wasn't the only time Sumner got arrested but it just seemed like even though they could catch him once in a while, they just couldn't figure out how to keep him in custody. The fact is, he talked his way out of it every time, and before they could blink, he was off to the next place, they (the *Federales*) knew not where.

Legend No. 6:

On another occasion, Sumner is passing out bibles in the area of his old adversary John Gaines. He's the ferry-boat owner who tried to stop the revival over near Milam and now he wants Sumner to stop passing out those bibles before he attracts the *Federales* and causes a confrontation. As the two men are discussing the pros and cons of bible distribution, another unique character in Texas history rides up to join in the discussion.

The name of this late arrival is Col. Pedro Elias Bean and the rest of this story could only happen in Texas with some kind of divine arrangement involved. *Señor* Bean is a full Colonel in the Mexican Army and he's out and about that day patrolling, doing what Army Officers do and wearing his Mexican Army Colonel's uniform. The unique thing is though, *"Bean"* is the only part of his name he was born with. He was actually called Peter Ellis Bean back in Tennessee when he was born there as an American citizen in June of 1783.

To make a really long story short, Bean had been taken prisoner by the Spanish in 1801 while he and some other young adventurers were on a filibustering (unauthorized warfare) expedition in Spanish Texas. He was taken deep into Mexico and incarcerated in various locations for the next ten years until finally he agrees to fight with the Spanish army against Mexican insurgents. But at the first opportunity he deserts the Spanish and joins up with the insurgents and by this time he's become more Mexican than American even to the point of forgetting a lot of his native English. Eventually the insurgents win, Mexico is granted independence and Mr. Pedro Elias Bean becomes a Colonel in the Mexican Army.[49]

You can't make this stuff up! When Col. Bean rides up to the two men discussing bible distribution, he wants to know what they're talking about and Mr. Gaines replies that he's defending law and order in his community because Rev. Bacon is trying to distribute bibles unlawfully. Sumner Bacon is caught red-handed with the bibles sure enough and figures he's on his way to the hoosegow again. But surprisingly, Col. Bean advises the pair that Rev. Bacon will be allowed to distribute all the bibles he wants to provided he doesn't disturb the peace. So, Mr. Gaines once again has to back down and leave Sumner to his work of preaching and distributing illegal bibles Score another one for Sumner Bacon in the most unlikely of ways.

Legend No. 7:

On another occasion Sumner was preaching in the Nacogdoches area and heard word being spread that he was going to be arrested. Believe it or not, some of the local Mexican soldiers had warned him this time so Sumner decided to turn himself in to the authorities before they pounced on him and made his life painful. As soon as they have him in custody and are confident that he can't get away again, they take him to the Commandant's office so that Sumner can finally be sentenced for all his misdeeds against the Mexican government. But who do you suppose is the presiding Commanding Officer on rotation that day? Why of course: it's none other than Col. Pedro Elias Bean who listens to the charges and rules that Preacher Bacon

---

[49] https://en.wikipedia.org/wiki/Peter_Ellis_Bean

can expound on the scriptures all he wants to...*as long as he doesn't disturb the peace.*

Legend No. 8:

In 1835, the fighting men of Texas began gathering together to start fighting against the Mexican Army as soon as things were ready. During that year the Rev. Sumner Bacon held a revival near San Augustine, Texas and some young ruffians try to break up his meeting. What they don't realize is that in the audience that night is none other than Colonel James Bowie who is one of those Texas fighting men and he has come to listen to the preaching. Cumberland leaders say later about the incident that Bowie had been *"deeply impressed with the simplicity and solemn earnestness"* of Sumner's message and he wanted to hear more of it.

According to many credible historians, Bowie tells the troublemakers in his uniquely persuasive manner, *"Col. Bowie is in command here today,"* at which point he takes this really large knife he's carrying and draws the sign of a large cross there on the ground. He then gestures to Sumner to continue the service and sits down to listen. The only sound in that place for the rest of the evening is the voice of Sumner Bacon preaching his heart out for the Kingdom of God in chorus with a lot of *"A-mens"* from the congregation that is now in full agreement with everything Sumner has to say. That particular revival lasted for several days and historians report that Col. Bowie was often in attendance. Of particular interest is the fact that there were no further disruptions.

Legend No. 9:

One day Sumner Bacon is riding his horse to an upcoming preaching engagement while in the company of a friend and co-worker in the ministry. Seemingly out of nowhere they are set upon by desperados with some really bad intentions. The outlaws outnumber the two men of God and soon knock Sumner unconscious whereupon the traveling companion, thinking Sumner dead, manages to regain control of his horse and escape. Soon enough the desperados observe Rev. Bacon regaining consciousness and communicate their plan to go ahead and finish him off once and for all.

But Sumner has faced this kind of challenge before and asks the desperados if he can pray one last prayer for them before they finish up their work. The outlaws agree releasing Sumner to drop to his knees, close his eyes and hold forth with a mighty prayer to the Almighty that lasts several minutes. When Sumner finally finishes praying and opens his eyes, the desperados are nowhere to be seen and have left behind a most convenient horse.

Simply Legendary

There are a lot more of these wonderful stories I could have included but these few examples should be enough for you to see that only a special man of God could have been involved in all of these events. It seems that God will use certain people to do impossible things as long as they are obedient people of faith who are willing to be led by the Holy Spirit. So, what these stories do is prove the presence of God in everything the Rev. Sumner Bacon put his hand to from 1826 until at least 1835. And as we'll see in later chapters, God's work with Sumner is far from over.

Another point to take away from these stories is that Sumner had developed an almost irresistible quality about his way of speaking. The man who previously spoke crudely and gruffly becomes, under the influence of the Holy Spirit, an energetic, passionate and persuasive speaker who seems to be able to always get his way. This quality is one of his principal abilities that make him a Legend.

The final point to take away is that somehow Sumner had been able to develop a lot of friends. People really liked him and wanted to help him succeed. Perhaps some of them had been his converts and maybe others had heard the stories about him as they began to come to light around the Territory. The man who for many years had no friends becomes under the influence of the Holy Spirit a man with friends seemingly everywhere as his fame spreads across the territory and all the way back to Arkansas, Louisiana and even Tennessee.

What we have here at the age of 45 is a genuine LEGEND ready for the next steps in his life which include Sumner Bacon _simultaneously_ going to war and starting a family. Well now, you wouldn't have expected him to go and do things the easy way, would you?

Therefore, prepare your minds for action.

1 Peter 1:13b

SIX: REV BACON PREPARES FOR WAR

As you've seen from the story so far, all during the time that Sumner Bacon was becoming a Texas Legend, he was working within an increasingly agitated political environment. The Mexican government had originally wanted Anglo settlers to come into Texas to help develop the territory, to secure the northern border and to provide a buffer between the Comanche Indians and the main part of Mexico to the south. But almost from the beginning the settlers were "unsettled" about life under Mexican control and began to voice their opposition to a number of issues that were interfering with the *"life, liberty and pursuit of happiness"* idea they'd been used to in the U.S. They also tended to steer clear of the Comanches and never did become that buffer.

When Sumner was arriving in Texas in 1828, he would have had little knowledge of the details of that environment but it wouldn't have taken him long to become an expert at it because that's what everybody was talking about. There were the Mexican authorities enforcing through their Army the 1824 Constitution. There were the Protestant Anglo settlers who were divided between those who wanted Protestant preachers to come in and those who didn't. There were Mexican settlers who were soon greatly outnumbered by the Anglos and with some exceptions tended to support the Mexican government. And there was the Catholic Church complaining about all the illegal preaching that was going on.

When Sumner starts his ministry, he's probably wanting to avoid political involvement as most ministers would, but of course by default he's included into the *pro-Protestant-*

pro-preaching group. In the beginning he would've tried to avoid talking about politics at his meetings, but the other political groups with the law on their side are determined to see to it that Sumner won't be able to fulfill what God has called him to do whether he talks about politics or not. From the get-go he finds himself personally involved in an explosive political environment he'd prefer not to be in because it puts him in conflict with a lot of people who need to hear his message but are closed to it for political reasons.

A Brief History Lesson

Now this settler agitation thing had pretty much gone on since the beginning of the land grant program in 1821. It tended to revolve around the absence of certain political rights those folks had previously been used to in the U.S. including the right of freedom of religion, the right to keep and bear arms and the right to trial by jury. Also, the Mexican government had failed to establish a system of public education which they had promised to the settlers. Also, Gen. Santa Anna had suspended the constitution in 1834 and made himself a dictator even though the settlers had been promised a representative republic. And on top of all that, the place where Texas *matters-of-state* took place was all the way down in the provincial-capital town of Saltillo and everything they did down there had to be done in Spanish.[50]

With all of these issues swirling and boiling across the territory, everything finally comes to a head in the latter part of 1835. Most folks say the actual revolution starts on October 2, 1835 when Texans repulse a detachment of

---

[50] The Influence of Christianity on Early Texas History, p.60-61

Mexican cavalry at the *Battle of Gonzalez*. Seven days later about 50 Texans storm the *Presidio at Goliad* and defeat a small detachment of Mexican defenders. After that to top off a really busy month, none other than Col. Jim Bowie with James Fannin and 90 Texas militia defeat 450 Mexican troops on October 28 at the *Battle of Concepcion* near San Antonio.[51]

And things don't slow down in November. On November 3rd, 1835 a *Consultation* (Convention) of Anglo English-speaking delegates is convened in San Antonio and it declares the right of Texans to form an independent government in view of Santa Anna's recent cancellation of the Mexican Constitution. Based on that resolution they establish a *provisional government* and then later in the month authorize the formation of the Texas Army commissioning Sam Houston as its commanding officer with the rank of Major General. There's also a battle on November 8th again led by Col. Jim Bowie which turns out to be yet another defeat for the Mexicans.[52]

But there's an even worse defeat that happens before the end of the year because on December 11, 1835 *General Martin Perfecto de Cos* surrenders the city of San Antonio to the new Texas Army making his brother-in-law *Generalissimo Santa Anna* furious and vowing vengeance on the *Texians* as soon as he can get his army in place.[53] The loss of San Antonio is an embarrassment to Mexico and Santa Anna is angry with his officers for what he feels is poor leadership in the field. The *Texians* on the other hand, buoyed by all their recent victories begin to think they will be able to take over the Territory in a cake walk.

---

[51] Ibid, pp. 60-62.
[52] https://en.wikipedia.org/wiki/Consultation_%28Texas%29
[53] https://en.wikipedia.org/wiki/Mart%C3%ADn_Perfecto_de_Cos

All the Mexican troops have been chased out of the Territory back to Mexico so it's just a matter of time. So confident are they after the San Antonio victory that some of the leaders of the Texas Army leave the battle field to return to their homes while others start talking about invading Mexico suddenly leaving Major General Sam Houston with a remnant of a leftover Army on his hands that needs to get prepared before a possible revenge-invasion by Santa Anna can get back to Texas.[54]

How Sumner Bacon gets Involved

It's important for the story that you're familiar with the highlights of this history because in that same latter part of 1835, Sumner suspends his traveling ministry, makes a trip back to Tennessee and returns in early 1836 to become actively involved in the struggle for independence. Suspending his ministry would've been a really big deal for him because he's fully committed to his calling and that means he would have concluded that he could no longer pursue it while what looked to be a full-fledged revolution was being stirred up all around him.

Not only then is 1835 a big year for Texas, it's also a big year for Sumner Bacon. Earlier in the year he'd finally been ordained in Louisiana by the *Cumberland Presbyterians* after years of trying only to now suspend his ministry a few months later. And according to the research, Sumner has been quietly involving himself all along with none other than the famous Sam Houston. Exactly how that came about isn't known for certain but we can make some assumptions based on the research and connecting some of the related time lines.

---

[54] Sam Houston...Hero of San Jacinto, TSHA 2016

The first thing to consider is that Mr. Houston first arrives in Texas in early December of 1832 and almost immediately gets involved in the political situation at the highest levels. That's surely because he's already famous as a result of his extensive political experience back in Tennessee including being a Representative to the U.S. Congress and the Governor of the State. In fact, he's a protégé and close associate of Andrew Jackson having served under him in the Army and also in the political arena. Keep in mind that Jackson had been elected U.S. President in 1829 and serves two terms until 1837. And, just so you know, not everybody in Texas likes President Jackson all that much which makes for an additional political division to add to the ones we've already talked about, plus it had a direct impact on the fate of certain other Texas heroes as we'll see a bit later.

When Houston arrives in Texas, he settles in Nacogdoches which is the eastern hub of Anglo-settler activity and located a mere 35 miles from San Augustine where Sumner maintains his headquarters. Houston quickly establishes a law practice and it's well-documented that Sumner traveled around and through the area of Nacogdoches on multiple occasions in the pursuit of his ministry. The fact is, in early 1833 he's returning to Texas as the *Bible Society's* new representative just when Houston is getting underway. Sumner Bacon is already a well-known resident in that area and in addition he's now the exclusive distributor of bibles for the entire Territory with an inventory of 2,000 units at his home base. It was inevitable then, probably unavoidable, that these two special characters would meet there in Nacogdoches, probably as early as the late spring of 1833, and discover that they're kindred spirits.

In support of that idea, they're almost the same age, Sumner is only three years older, and they share similar backgrounds. Sumner had left home in 1810 and Sam Houston ran away from home in 1809. Sumner had become a wilderness man on his travels down to Arkansas. Sam had become a wilderness man living with the Cherokee Indians on two separate occasions. In fact, he'd even been adopted by them and given the Indian name *"Raven."* In sum, these were two similarly tough characters who had the ability to gravitate between the wilderness and regular folks when they needed to. Since Houston was probably not yet a serious believer, it would've been a challenge to the Evangelist Sumner Bacon to share the gospel with such a famous man and I have no doubt that he tried it, probably more than once!

From early 1833 until the latter part of 1835, Sam Houston is working increasingly on his political activities and Sumner Bacon is on the move preaching and distributing bibles mostly in that same vicinity of East Texas. Of course, Sumner had traveled all over the Territory during the previous five years and knows his way around more than most. At some point, in addition to his ministry, Sumner starts acting as a courier for Mr. Houston, maybe occasionally at the beginning but more frequently as the political situation intensifies and it becomes increasingly more inevitable that war is in their future. And so, during the latter part of 1835 Sumner temporarily suspends his ministry responding it seems to several compelling factors:

☐ It's fairly obvious that a war is coming and Sumner sees that he won't be able to conduct his camp meetings during a war.

☐ Secondly, he wants to continue working as a courier for Sam Houston so he can be involved in the war effort in a way that won't have him shooting people.

☐ Thirdly, I believe Sam Houston wants to send Sumner on a secret courier mission to Tennessee to request military assistance from Houston's long-time friend General R. G. Dunlap.

☐ Finally, I believe Sumner already has a love interest back in Tennessee, and when all these events come together, he concludes that the trip to Tennessee in late 1835 is an opportune time to get married if he can convince a certain young lady there to come back to Texas as his wife.

That's when Sumner takes what for him is the radical step of suspending his ministry. But he has every intention of resuming it as soon as events permit and he makes everyone aware of that including Sam Houston and the certain young lady waiting in Tennessee. I assure you as a minister myself that Sumner's calling is his first concern and priority and he didn't formally suspend his ministry without giving it a lot of thought and prayer.

Sumner Bacon and His Special Missions

Now one of the really interesting parts of this story is that on several occasions General Houston sent Sumner on some very special missions. They were highly important and would've been reserved for a special intermediary whose judgment and perseverance could be trusted and who was familiar with the area to be traveled. Keep in mind that in 1835 it would be a decade or more before the telegraph becomes operational in the U.S.[55] and the Pony Express is still 15 years in the future.[56] Also, the fledgling U.S. train industry is decades away from reaching the frontier areas. [57] So, the only way to get important messages to far away destinations and people as quickly as possible is by special wilderness-tested men on horseback.

All these years later only God knows all the details about Sumner's secret missions because most of the related documentation has either been lost or never existed. But, based on the research that we ARE able to find, we can put together some logical theories. It's well documented that after Texas had won its independence, Houston sent Sumner to Tennessee in July of 1836[58] on a secret mission to seek military aid through his long-time friend General R. G. Dunlap. Houston was concerned that the Mexican Army would regroup and come back to Texas for another try at recovering their former Territory. But the documentation that has been preserved clearly indicates that there had been a PREVIOUS request for assistance that General Dunlap hadn't yet been able to arrange. Since it was Sumner Bacon who made the documented trip following independence to meet with General Dunlap, it's very likely that it was the same Sumner Bacon who made the previous trip late 1835 before independence. The only fact we're not able to tie down is exactly when that previous trip was made.

---

[55] https://en.wikipedia.org/wiki/Electrical_telegraph

[56] https://www.google.com/search?q=History+of+the+Pony+Express&ie=utf-8&oe=utf-8

[57] https://en.wikipedia.org/wiki/Oldest_railroads_in_North_America

[58] https://www.tshaonline.org/supsites/nance-backup/jn_015.html

Sumner Bacon was the perfect courier/intermediary for these assignments. He was responsible, tough and courageous and he was an experienced frontier traveler. He would've already become familiar with certain parts of Tennessee during his wilderness days on the way down to Arkansas and also by making the trip up there in 1832-33 to pick up the bibles from the *American Bible Society*. Keep in mind also that Sam Houston was from the State of Tennessee, had once been its Governor and still knows a lot of people in high places including his friend General Dunlap. As it happens, the General is also stationed in Nashville, Tennessee not far from the headquarters of the *Cumberland Presbyterians* and the local operation of the *American Bible Society*.

From the available documentation we know that Sumner traveled to that area in the latter part of 1835 after he suspended his ministry. He was there ostensibly to court a certain young lady and it will probably not surprise you to learn that the young lady lives in a small community that is *"coincidentally"* VERY close to... *Nashville, Tennessee!*

Why could Sumner not have had a dual purpose for his trip to Tennessee in late 1835: to secretly deliver Houston's documented previous attempt to secure military assistance and to simultaneously court the young lady? Sam Houston was looking for help to fight what he saw to be an eventual inevitable war against Mexico that he believed was coming soon and Sumner Bacon was going to Tennessee anyway on another mission. This would've been a perfect arrangement because the request for military assistance had to be discrete since the official position of the U.S. government throughout the Texas struggle for independence was neutrality. Sumner Bacon's trip there to go a-courting would have been a perfect cover!

I believe the probability is very high that Sam Houston's original request for volunteer military assistance was delivered by the Rev. Sumner Bacon direct to General Dunlap probably at his residence near Nashville, Tennessee during the latter part of 1835. Once he had delivered that message along with any accompanying commentary, he was ready to address the second objective of his journey. And by the way, it's approximately 650 miles from his home in San Augustine, Texas to Nashville, Tennessee.

Sumner Bacon Starts a Family

Now you would think that Sumner would've had enough to do getting ready to go to war. But as he's about to turn 46 years of age, it occurs to him that this would be a good time while he's on a trip to Tennessee to finally get married. What better time than when a war may be going on by the time he returns so he can have something challenging to do! Knowing Sumner as we now do, it never occurs to him that he might get himself killed in that war and leave behind a new wife. And so, we find our friend Sumner getting married to Miss Elizabeth McKerall in mid-January of 1836 [59] in Spring Hill, Maury County, Tennessee which is about 35 miles as the crow flies from...*Nashville, Tennessee*!

Everything Sumner is doing in his life now traces back to either East Texas or Nashville, Tennessee including: his church denomination headquarters, his bible supply

---

[59] http://www.findagrave.com/cgi-bin/fg.cgi?page=gr&GRid=24714922

source, his contact with a future provider of military assistance, and the place where his friend and now courier-boss Sam Houston had formerly served as Tennessee Governor. And oh yes, Nashville had been the capital of Tennessee since 1826 [60] and Houston had become Governor in 1827.[61] And of course, the home of Sumner's future wife is there too.

The main question remaining is this: how did Sumner get connected with Miss McKerall well enough that a trip to her area in late 1835 would include a stop-off in Spring Hill, Tennessee for a wedding? How did that happen? There isn't any documentation about it so we're going to have to make some more educated assumptions from the information we *do* have and go from there. Fortunately, it won't be all that difficult.

The first thing we need to confirm is that Miss McKerall was born in 1810 which is the same year Sumner left home in Massachusetts. That makes her 25 years of age at the end of 1835 when Sumner is arriving in Tennessee. Sumner was born in January of 1790 so he's almost 46 years of age when he's trying to arrange their marriage. But how did they get to know each other?

Do you remember that Sumner returned to Arkansas toward the end of 1832 and that he met up with Rev. Benjamin Chase to receive the appointment as the first representative to Texas for the *American Bible Society?* And that afterwards, Sumner had to go up to his denomination's home base in Burns. Tennessee to arrange to pick up all those bibles? All of that was happening in

---

[60] http://web.utk.edu/~rsmeltze/IT/IT575/eportfolio/exerI.html
[61] https://www.google.com/search?q=When+was+Sam+Houston+the+Governor+of+Tennessee&ie=utf-8&oe=utf-8

the tight proximity of Nashville. If the two of them met up on that trip, Miss McKerall was 19 or 20 years old and they begin at that time a long-distance courtship that culminates in their wedding in January of 1836. During those intervening years it's entirely possible that Sumner Bacon took a trip or two back to that area or that he somehow corresponded with Miss McKerall to convey his intentions even though he was by all accounts limited in his writing skills.

Of course, it's not outside the realm of possibility that Sumner meets her for the first time in late 1835 and sweeps his future wife off her feet over a few weeks with his persuasive way of speaking. But that would be the less likely of the two options given the ways of courtship and marriage at that time in our history.

Soon after the marriage, the two newlyweds start their 650-mile trip back to San Augustine, Texas. Apparently, they spend a little time together before the war resumes and the new Mrs. Bacon would have been challenged to not only get acquainted with her new surroundings in Texas - which was a far cry from the area near Nashville, Tennessee - but also to get to know her new husband. How long had they really known each other? Had she fully understood that she was marrying a tough wilderness-man-minister who put his life at risk every time he went somewhere to preach and win souls? Had she understood fully that she was marrying a man who was going to be involved in a war at the highest levels including the likes of Major General Sam Houston who had been the Governor of her home state when she was a teenager?

A key take-away from this chapter is that clearly Sumner becomes directly involved in the struggle for Texas independence primarily <u>as a result of</u> getting to know Sam Houston. We need to also keep in mind that he knew Jim Bowie as well who was a high-level officer in the Texas Army and in addition, he would have been well acquainted with any of the other "rebel" leaders who were living in that same part of East Texas.

And finally, there is the point that Sumner Bacon, called to preach a Protestant Gospel, was by unavoidable default a part of the political group that was leading the resistance against the Mexican government. What secular historians tend to miss is that the matter of religion was at the core of the resistance and served as the principal basis that defined the "political" divisions among the parties to the war.

As the Bacons arrive in St. Augustine, the war looms in the immediate future and almost immediately Sumner leaves his new wife in the care of a local friend and neighbor Rev. Samuel McMahon, a Methodist minister who had moved to San Augustine in 1831. It is most interesting that Rev. McMahon's wife was originally from Maury County, Tennessee which as we now know was also the home of the new Mrs. Elizabeth McKerall Bacon.[62] Do you suppose that the Rev. and Mrs. McMahon had had anything to do with matchmaking their friend Sumner Bacon to a young attractive lady they had known back in Tennessee? Historical detective work is fascinating!

And so, Sumner deposits his new wife with the McMahon's and off he goes to rejoin the struggle for Texas independence. [63]He will look for Sam Houston to report for

---

[62] http://archives.gcah.org/xmlui/bitstream/handle/10516/1596/MH-1970-10-Vernon-48-54.pdf?sequence=1

[63] "Pistol Packing Preachers" by Barbara Barton, p. 18

courier duty and so he can be debriefed on his recent trip to Nashville. His ministry is temporarily suspended and in the midst of the winter of 1836, he's now ready, new wife and all, to enter into the struggle to secure independence for his adopted homeland.

There is an appointed time for everything…a time for war and a time for peace.

Ecclesiastes 3:1, 8b

SEVEN: REV BACON GOES TO WAR

The tumultuous year of 1836 turns out to be the precise *moment* in God's timing when everything changes. It changes because of a series of particular events that later on will be the most remembered part of the Territory's history. Certainly, great events come later, but the ones that are first remembered, the ones that are first honored, the ones that are first passed on to succeeding generations are the events of 1836.

The backdrop is that the Texas Territory that had "belonged" to Spain for 302 years had only been under Mexican control for 15 when the majority of its occupants became so dissatisfied with their government that they decided to pursue something new. Mexico had gained its independence from Spain in 1821 through armed revolt and had attempted an ambitious experiment for development of the territory by encouraging the immigration of Anglo settlers from the United States. The experiment failed because it turned out that the immigrants weren't interested in being assimilated into the existing Spanish/Mexican culture. They came with a different language, a different view of Christianity, a different legal system and a different form of government.

As 1836 dawns in Texas, Sumner is off in Tennessee getting married, but Sam Houston is focusing on an unexpected and potentially devastating situation that develops with the new *Provisional Government* that had only just been established a couple of months before at the *Consultation* of November 3. Houston had been made commanding officer of the Texas Army and his main responsibility had been to take charge and prepare for future battles. But in the following month of December, the Mexican Army had been soundly defeated and had to surrender San Antonio. That victory for the settlers caused the retreat of the entire Mexican Army back to Mexico and to reiterate, it left the rebels way over confident about their future. Many Anglo *Texian* fighting men thought the war was over and went home for Christmas or off to invade Mexico leaving a somewhat disorganized remnant of a Texas Army that General Houston would have to rebuild.[64]

The Matamoros Expedition

So over confident had they become that certain leaders of the *Provisional Government,* driven largely by economic concerns that were related to personal investments and land speculation, had decided by mid-December 1835 to invade Mexico. A campaign was put together a few weeks later and it developed into a major event in Texas history called the *Matamoros Expedition.* The fact is though, it almost wound up giving Texas back to Mexico.[65]

To make a long story short, those provisional leaders ordered General Houston on December 17 to send a force of more than 200 men to capture the town of Matamoros down in Mexico just across the *Rio Grande River* from Brownsville, Texas. But before it can happen, the leadership becomes divided over whether or not it's a good strategy. Houston realizes right away that what he's been ordered to do isn't prudent and begins talking the men out of going on the expedition. He rightly expects Santa Anna to mount an offensive in the near future to retake their

---

[64] https://tshaonline.org/handbook/online/articles/qdm01
[65] https://en.wikipedia.org/wiki/Matamoros_Expedition

lost territory and he figures he'll need every fighting settler he can find. In other words, Houston feels they don't need to be taking the fight to Mexico when for all they know its superior army may already be making its way back into the Territory.

General Houston succeeds in convincing more than half the contingent to abandon the expedition but the remaining group continues on anyway. On the way they strip the Alamo and Goliad garrisons of all their small arms and supplies, ignore Houston's authority as commanding general and split the *Provisional Government* into opposing groups: pro-Matamoros invasion or against. They don't realize it yet but the split will soon make it necessary to form yet another new government.

After much dissention, the contingent finally meets up with General Jose de Urrea in San Patricio (near Corpus Christi) on February 27, 1836 and they wind up getting themselves decisively defeated with their main leader killed in action and most of the troops killed or wounded. It's a disaster that proves to be a major factor in the events leading to the defeat of the Texas forces not only at the battle of San Patricio but also at the soon coming battles of Agua Dulce Creek (March 2), The Alamo (March 6), Refugio (March 15), Coleto (March 19), Port Copano (March 21) and a particularly disastrous event at Goliad (March 27). In short, the year 1836 didn't start off nearly as well as 1835 had ended.

And so, Sumner Bacon returns to Texas in early to mid-February following his wedding in Tennessee only to find his adopted homeland in disarray, the Army depleted or off on the boondoggle to Matamoros (where they never got to), the government divided and on the verge of collapse and General Sam Houston off on a self-imposed "furlough." Frustrated and disgusted with the *Provisional Government,* Houston nonetheless uses his time constructively to negotiate a new treaty with the Cherokee Indians of East Texas so they won't fight in support of the Mexican Army in the future. Sumner's surely amazed at how much things have changed in the short time he's been away!

Time for a New Strategy

The first thing Sumner does when he arrives back in Texas is deposit his new wife in the McMahon home and the second thing is to kiss her goodbye and renew assurances he'll return safely after the war. Then he goes looking for his friend General Sam Houston.

There's an urgency driving him, a sense that something will soon be changing. He's keenly aware that Houston is *the* one man in the territory that God has provided to lead them to victory and freedom. His ministry has been set aside for the moment and will remain suspended until after the war. And so, Sumner Bacon makes himself available and he does it with the same passion, the same determination and the same confidence that have so characterized his life since that special night in Arkansas 10 years before when he came to know Jesus.

It takes a day or two for Sumner to locate Houston and report for duty. The first thing Houston does after filling Sumner in on all the latest developments and debriefing him on his trip to see General Dunlap is to officially appoint him to the position of *Texas Army Chaplain.* The second is to instruct him to stand by for the imminent resumption of his courier job as the *Matamoros Expedition* works towards its expected failure in the near future. Houston sees it as inevitable but no one's anticipating the total collapse that's actually on the way.

Fortunately, 1836 is a Leap Year, so February has 29 days and they will need every day of it to prepare for the Mexican Army. In fact, word soon comes that General Santa Anna has crossed the Rio Grande River on February 16 and General Jose de Urrea crosses the next day. So, the Mexican Army in two large contingents is back in Texas. And, despite reports from a number of sources that Santa Anna is continuing on his way to San Antonio, the commanding officer of the Alamo, Colonel William B. Travis refuses to believe those reports and plans for an arrival no earlier than mid-March.[66]

But General Houston is of a different mind about the timing and rightly figures that the Mexican Army will move against San Antonio sooner. So, he sends Sumner with desperate dispatches to both the Alamo in San Antonio and to the garrison in Goliad on several occasions to warn the troops to abandon those locations as indefensible so they can work toward consolidating their assets for a more favorable setting in the future. Colonel Travis disregards Houston's orders and keeps trying to fortify the Alamo and make a defense. It's also documented that Sumner is sent to Victoria, Texas with dispatches which probably had to do more with trying to impede the *Matamoros Expedition* than anything else.

Meanwhile, General Santa Anna implements what starts out as an effective strategy: he sends General Urrea to meet the *Matamoros Expedition* while he heads with his

---

[66] https://en.wikipedia.org/wiki/Timeline_of_the_Texas_Revolution
http://samhoustonmemorialmuseum.com/history/

contingent directly to the Alamo. Six days later on February 23 Santa Anna arrives in San Antonio and puts the Alamo under siege with his artillery. He has arrived at least three weeks earlier than Colonel Travis expects and they're NOT ready to face the 1,500 Mexican soldiers they see just outside their now famous Spanish mission. There are only 156 *Texian* fighting men present that day and as the Mexican Army hurries to get in position, the resident *Texian Army* is scouring the nearby countryside in a last second dash to bring in food and supplies. They have some Mexican muskets to defend themselves with but almost no powder for their cannons.[67]

Now among the Texian fighting men in the Alamo, there are three that will become famous and you can find out more about them in Appendix One. One of them is Colonel James Bowie. He arrives in the Alamo on January 19 before Col. Travis arrives and is named second in command to the then commanding officer James C. Neill. Keep in mind that General Houston had ordered them to abandon the Alamo and burn its contents as they were leaving. But Colonel Bowie makes his home in San Antonio. He'd married the mayor's daughter there in 1831 and had two children with her before they all died along with his wife's parents in a cholera epidemic in 1833.[68] He didn't want the Mexicans to retake San Antonio and decided with Neill to disregard General Houston's orders and stay to defend the Alamo. The day that Santa Anna arrives to lay siege to the Alamo, James Bowie comes down with a debilitating sickness that forces him into bed for the duration of the battle.

---

[67] https://en.wikipedia.org/wiki/Timeline_of_the_Texas_Revolution
[68] https://en.wikipedia.org/wiki/James_Bowie

The second famous occupant is Colonel William Travis who arrives in the Alamo on February 3 and immediately has a confrontation with James Bowie over who has authority as second in command. Eight days later, Neill leaves because of a death in his family and appoints Travis as commanding officer, much to the objection of James Bowie. In a couple of days, the two decide to split the commanding officer role with Travis over the regular Army troops and Bowie in charge of the volunteers. Travis joins with the strategy to defend the Alamo instead of obeying Houston and significantly misjudges the urgency of their situation.

The third famous occupant is David Crockett who arrives in the Alamo on February 8. He had crossed into Texas during the first few days of January 1836 and chooses to join Travis in the Alamo. The alternative of joining up with Sam Houston would have put him with a well-known protégé of his long-time political nemesis, President Andrew Jackson.[69] David Crockett is in Texas for scarcely two months in total having come here to start a new life and leave behind his political disappointments and rivalry with Jackson. He becomes a legendary hero, forever a part of Texas history, because he makes the wrong choice and stays to defend the Alamo.

Sumner Bacon knows all of them from his courier trips to the Alamo. He gives them General Houston's warnings and orders to abandon the Alamo. He knows James Bowie particularly well but the lines of authority had broken down. The fighting men in the Alamo weren't listening to General Houston any more. There were cannons in the Alamo and many historians say that there was no way to

---

[69]http://www.tamu.edu/faculty/ccbn/dewitt/adp/history/bios/crockett/crockett.html

remove them as Houston had ordered in the remaining time. They have waited too long. So, they choose to stay and protect the cannons even though they have no cannon powder since it had all been commandeered by the Matamoros folks. Before the end comes, a few more men are able to join with the little group of defenders making a force of about 185 fighting against 1500 motivated Mexican regular army troops.

On February 29, Sam Houston arrives in the town of *"Washington on the Brazos"* to attend the *Convention of 1836*. The Convention will start the next day and has as its two main purposes to terminate the *Provisional Government* that had never worked out and to declare the *Republic of Texas* once and for all totally separated from Mexico. The next day the Convention is convened and on the following day March 2, which happens to be Sam Houston's forty-third birthday, a *Declaration of Independence* is officially declared which makes Santa Anna apoplectic a few days later when he hears about it. On that same day Sam Houston becomes a signer of the *Declaration* and on March 4, 1836 he's officially appointed as Commander of all Texan Forces.

One of the interesting things to remember about the *Convention* is that it only took one day for a select committee to come up with a finished *Declaration* that the Convention could vote on and adopt. That's because certain of the leaders had come to the meeting with the document already largely prepared. Basically, they only had to perform some editing and issue the final document. And while they were at it, they elected an interim President to head up their new government: David G. Burnet. He will be replaced the following October by the first popularly elected President of the new republic: General Sam Houston.

You can see a copy of the *Declaration* in Appendix Two and one thing you'll notice is that it's a list of complaints against the government of Mexico to explain why the signers are declaring their separation. Many Texans don't realize that Complaint #16 is a declaration against mandated religion and in support of religious freedom. It reads as follows:

It (the Mexican government) denies us the right of worshipping the Almighty according to the dictates of our own consciences, by the support of a national religion calculated to promote the temporal interests of its human functionaries rather than the glory of the true and living God.

Let it be clear that the majority of the people who had come to Texas in response to the Spanish and Mexican land grant programs were no longer willing to live under religious tyranny. They wanted all residents of Texas to be free to worship as they pleased, Catholic and Protestant alike, and the *Declaration* of March 2, 1836 intended to establish that freedom for all time. Dedicated men of God like Sumner Bacon had come to Texas illegally by man's law, risking life and limb to preach and teach the Word according to God's Law. The culmination of their influence can be found clearly stated in Complaint #16 of the *Texas Declaration of Independence.*

Meanwhile, the Alamo is still under siege and will finally fall after a valiant defense just four days later on March 6. They had held out for thirteen days with no cannon powder against vastly superior forces. True to their flag of "No Quarter," the Mexican Army killed any of the *Texian* fighting men they found still living including the wounded.

And they burned all the bodies on a huge pyre instead of burying them or leaving them for their loved ones to care for.

The Mexican Army won the battle that day but the way they conducted themselves at the end created anger across the territory. In fact, it served to bring the different political factions together into a more unified resistance determined now to defeat their common enemy and establish a new country.

Houston leaves the *Convention* to take charge of the *Army of the Republic of Texas* and upon hearing of the fall of the Alamo initiates a *"retreat, consolidate and prepare"* military strategy. As an experienced military man, he knows it's the ONLY possible route to eventual victory. He also sends Sumner Bacon on an urgent mission to New Orleans to purchase powder for however many cannons they may still be able to find because they will need them someday when the time is right and the odds are more favorable. They aren't ready yet to win the War and take command of their new country, and Sam Houston sees this more keenly than anyone else. As Sumner prepares to leave, it is said that Sam Houston gives him one last instruction to emphasize the urgency: *"Now Brother Bacon: long rides and short prayers!"*[70]

His special courier proves to be a man of many abilities and his assignment for procuring cannon powder will show that he's also now a man of substance who's willing to commit whatever he possesses to the future of the Texas Republic. He DOES purchase that cannon powder and he buys it with $561.00 of his own money on behalf of the

---

[70] "Pistol Packing Preachers" by Barbara Barton, p. 20

new republic.[71] That amount would be worth at least $15,000.00 in today's dollars which would be a goodly amount for most people in this day and age to be giving away all at one time.[72] Fifty days after the declaration of the new republic, a battle will be fought that succeeds in bringing forth a new nation with a great destiny. The cannon powder that the Texas Army will use in that decisive battle will have been purchased with the personal funds of a feisty, determined, indefatigable Presbyterian evangelist who refuses to be defeated.

The Last Straw

Obviously, the month of March 1836 was not a good time for the new Republic even though they successfully installed a new government. There was a series of seven consecutive defeats including the Alamo that started on February 27 and went on through the entire month of March. But one of those defeats, the last one which occurs on March 27 is a particular event in never-forgotten Texas history that's the *final straw*. It's the day the Mexican Army goes too far across an important line of decency.

If the Alamo defeat was a unifier of the people, the events at Goliad were the catalyst that propelled the new republic to victory over a superior fighting force. It is one thing to fight a war and win victories or suffer defeats. Men are wounded or killed but many live through their defeats to fight another day. It's another thing entirely to ignore the unofficial codes of honor that govern "civilized" warfare. To be sure, each side is trying to win the battle of the moment and avoid being killed themselves. But on both sides, there

---

[71] http://www.texashighways.com/eat/item/6194-bacon-146-s-bibles
[72] https://www.measuringworth.com/m/calculators/uscompare/result.php?year_source=1836&amount=561&year_result=2016

are human beings involved and they have homes and children and dreams and hopes that should never be dishonored. We may defeat someone but we should never dishonor them. Perhaps we can even find a way to grieve with them, sorrowing for their losses and humiliation because that's what Jesus would do.

There's noble warfare and there's a defiling warfare. The latter kind hurts the one committing the dishonor much more than the one who loses the battle. In their frustration the Mexican Army officers led by General Santa Anna cross a line of decency and honor that fuels a reaction completely opposite to what they had wanted.

With the territory still angry over the events that occurred in the Alamo, the most controversial event of the war, referred to in history as the *Goliad Massacre,* takes place just three weeks later. In the several days leading up to it, a number of *Texian Army* soldiers had been forced to surrender to the Mexican Army who were far better equipped. Included with those who surrendered was the commanding officer of the Goliad garrison, Col. James Fannin who believed that those who were surrendering would be held for a short time and then released into the United States. But that's not what happened. When more than 425 of the surrendered *Texians* had been accumulated at *Fort Defiance* in Goliad, General Santa Anna ordered their execution and the bodies burned. In the ensuing melee, 28 of the condemned men managed to escape after feigning death so that the story could be told.[73] Their story revealed the manner of the executions and about how many of the *Texians* had been clubbed and stabbed to death. It told of how Col. Fannin had been shot

---

[73] https://en.wikipedia.org/wiki/Goliad_massacre

in the face while forced to sit in a chair and how all the bodies had been stacked up and burned like at the Alamo.

When the details of the *Massacre* get out there's an even greater outpouring of anger among the Anglo community and it ignites a strong and immediate reaction. Suddenly, hundreds of new *Texian* volunteers come running to join Houston's Texas Army. Many of them had been on the fence before, not sure that outright rebellion against Mexico was the smart thing to do. They're no longer on the fence. This reaction to the dishonorable conduct of the Mexican Army is the main thing that produces eventual victory for the *Texian Army.* It also generates a bitter animosity from a future neighboring country that becomes the 28th state in the U.S. That animosity is to last for more than a century. Goliad was the last straw!

In the days just before or just after the *Massacre,* Sumner returns to Texas from New Orleans with cannon powder in hand too late for Goliad but just in time for the battle to come. General Houston puts that powder under the command of Lt. Col. James Clinton Neill whose job is to assemble the new artillery corps. That's the same James Neill who had been the commanding officer of the Alamo before being replaced by Col. William Travis during the days just before the battle. Houston now has an Army, they have cannons with more on the way, they have Sumner's cannon powder and they're training for battle, all the while retreating and avoiding battles they can't win because they're not yet ready. There's a lot of criticism about so much retreating because people are angry and want to fight. General Houston though wants to win...*and he wants to win big*!

A Most Decisive Rematch

For the three weeks following the *Massacre*, the Texas Army stays away from confrontations with the larger Mexican contingents and concentrates on training all the new troops. For two of those three weeks they're able to make camp at *Groce's Landing* on the west side of the Brazos River and get some rest while they train.

On April 11 they receive the famous *Twin Sisters* cannons fabricated in Ohio and shipped through New Orleans to arrive just at the right moment (see Appendix Three for more about the *Twin Sisters*). While this is going on, Sumner Bacon is performing his courier work and a lot of that communication is between General Houston and the leaders of the new government who want Houston to make a stand and fight. Like most government bureau-crats they have no idea how to actually fight a war and, in this case, they can't seem to comprehend that there may be as many as four thousand or more Mexican troops already inside Texas. Those troops would like nothing better than to find and fight the greatly outnumbered Texas Army and bring the rebellion to a swift and final end. Houston has less than one thousand mostly NEW troops presently assembled, so you can see the problem.

On April 15 Houston breaks camp and begins to move on. The next day he crosses the Brazos River and on April 18 arrives in Harrisburg, Texas. On that same day the providence of God is revealed when Deaf Smith and Henry Karnes capture a Mexican courier carrying intelligence about the locations and future plans of all the Mexican troops in the Territory. From that intelligence Houston realizes that Santa Anna has a relatively small force presently with him and that they aren't far away. So, like most great generals leading their men, the next thing he does is give a rousing, encouraging speech. He tells his Army that they will soon be in the battle and that when they fight, they should *"Remember the Alamo"* and *"Remember Goliad."*

They fight a couple of small skirmishes but keep moving toward the targeted contingent of the Mexican Army. Santa Anna has only about 700 troops with him, Houston has more than 900. On the morning of April 21, Santa Anna receives reinforcements of more than 500 additional troops and Houston has the bridge burned they had crossed over on so that no additional reinforcements will be able to get through easily into the otherwise isolated area that both armies have marched into. Now with the bridge burned, whichever side is defeated won't be able to escape easily because it will have to go through almost impassable marshes and wetlands. It's shaping up as a fight to the finish.

Santa Anna has chosen a camp site in a place called *San Jacinto* that's too vulnerable and he's highly criticized for that by his troops. Houston sees the mistake, burns the bridge and has an appropriate attack plan that he shares with his leading officers. The two camps are only 500 yards apart and Santa Anna expects Houston to attack during the morning of April 21. But the attack doesn't come.

Later in the day around 3:30 PM the attack DOES come and it comes while the Mexican troops are still in siesta time. They have failed to post a guard thinking that since the battle didn't commence in the morning, they can wait until the following day and expect Houston to attack during the morning of April 22. In eighteen minutes on Thursday afternoon April 21, the Mexican Army of more than 1,200 is decimated in what historians call one of the most decisive military battles in the history of the world.[74] Indeed, 650 of the Mexican soldiers are killed and 300 captured. The other 300 escape running in full-fledged retreat through the marshes and bayous of southeast Texas. The *Texians* chase them and all the while they're yelling: *Remember the Alamo, remember Goliad!* They chase them until it's too dark, which is the only reason 300 get away through the mud and the marshes and the bayous. In comparison the *Texian* side suffers 11 deaths and 30 wounded including Sam Houston whose ankle has been shattered by a rifle ball. The next day Santa Anna himself is captured hiding in a Private's uniform in a marsh area near the burned-out bridge [75] by James Sylvester and his search party of *Texian* fighters. [76] Houston has won his big battle!

An Unlikely Postscript

One of the things that most present-day Texans don't fully consider when we celebrate our history is that a God-ordained destiny was also involved in the events that happened AFTER the famous battle at *San Jacinto* just as much as before. Otherwise, it could have easily gone a different way. After all, there were still at least 2,500 Mexican troops in Texas, maybe more, that could have theoretically overwhelmed the little *Texian Army* if they had only mounted a counter offensive. But quite often when there are charismatic dictatorial-type leaders in control such as General Santa Anna, the people under

---

[74] http://www.tamu.edu/faculty/ccbn/dewitt/batsanjacinto.htm
[75] https://en.wikipedia.org/wiki/Battle_of_San_Jacinto
    https://tshaonline.org/handbook/online/articles/qes04
[76] http://www.poblar.com/texashistory/historysummary.htm

them don't function well with unexpectedly-acquired responsibility.

When the word comes that Santa Anna has been captured, the remaining leaders DO get together to talk about a counter-offensive. But without their leader, they aren't able to agree on a battle plan. Some of the generals want to fight but others are demoralized and want to start a gradual retreat back to Mexico. For the moment they're paralyzed, indecisive, not knowing what the General would want them to do. Meanwhile, it doesn't take the *Texians* very long to figure out that the man they captured near the burned-out bridge in a private's uniform is none other than the Mexican President and Supreme General, Santa Anna. They find out about it because when the other captured troops first see him in *Texian* hands, they call out to him *"presidente"* and it's a *"dead giveaway."* Once Houston realizes who they've captured, the negotiating begins and Santa Anna is eager to trade some treaties and concessions for his life.

General Houston is a very smart military man but what he does next is simply brilliant. He knows that there are many more Mexican troops in Texas probably getting together at that very moment to organize and mount a counter-offensive. And, he knows that if that happens, he's significantly outmanned and, having decisively won the battle at San Jacinto, he could still lose the War if he makes a wrong move now. He's also lying under a tree severely wounded with a shattered ankle. So, he offers to spare Santa Anna's life in exchange for some peace treaties including a special dispatch to be delivered immediately back to the remaining Mexican Army. The dispatch signed by *"el presidente"* reads as follows:

"I have agreed with General Houston for an armistice (peace treaty) and the war will cease forever."

When the other generals receive that dispatch, they decide to start moving south, not toward a counter-offensive but in a slow retreat back to Mexico. Finally on June 15 they cross the *Rio Grande River* and they don't come back to Texas in full force as an organized Army for six years.[77] The fact is they won't be able to come back for a while because they find so much civil unrest in Mexico when they get back there that the Army has to be on constant alert to keep things from breaking out into an all-out overthrow of the government.

General Houston doesn't know all this of course. He knows the Army has gone back to Mexico but he believes they will return soon to mount that counter-offensive. So, he sends Sumner Bacon back to Tennessee in July to follow up with General Dunlap. Eventually a couple of thousand mercenary troops DO arrive in Texas along with thousands of people coming from the U.S. who want to be a part of raising up the new country. In fact, there are so many people wanting to join the *Texian Army* that General Houston is temporarily challenged to accommodate them all and some even have to be turned away.

Sometimes the hand of God on something isn't apparent until we take some extra time to look for it. People will always try to take credit for what God does. Santa Anna, an experienced military man chooses a vulnerable spot to make camp, Houston burns a bridge, the Mexican Army takes inopportune siestas, two special long-awaited cannons arrive a mere ten days before the battle so the

---

[77] See Appendix Five in this publication about the Mexican Invasion of 1842.

Texians have some functioning artillery, Sumner Bacon brings back cannon powder just in time, Santa Anna is captured, Houston has the idea of sending a dispatch from the vanquished Mexican general back to his army generals and there's an armed uprising going on back in Mexico when the Army gets back there. That's a lot of coincidence, in fact too much for it to be coincidence! The evidence of God is everywhere around us if we'll just look for it! In this case everything works to cancel out the idea of a counter offensive which gives the new country a little breathing room to get started.

General Santa Anna is eventually sent to Washington D.C. still in captivity where he meets with President Andrew Jackson and promises to stop making trouble. He finally arrives back in Mexico on February 23, 1837 and heads to his presidential *"rancho"* where he announces his retirement from public life. While he was away, he's been deposed and is soon replaced by an old enemy, Anastasio Bustamante who wants to send an army back to Texas. But he finds an empty treasury in Mexico City and all that local trouble he has to deal with instead. The recovery of *Tejas* will have to wait for another day.[78]

By that time, the new Republic has become established. They have a real Army and Sam Houston is the country's first President. Sumner Bacon is back from Tennessee to resume his ministry in his new country and to settle down with his new wife. All during the war Sumner has performed continuous courier missions for General Houston. The documentation mentions only a few of his most noteworthy missions but there are ongoing assignments including some for a short time after the war

---

[78] See Appendix Four in this publication for a most interesting story.

ends. If he had been intercepted and captured during the war, he would most likely have been executed as a spy. Or, he might have talked his way out of it or God would've sent some *"legendary"* means of escape.

Even though there's no documentation about his work as an Army Chaplain, we do know he was appointed to that position at the beginning of the conflict. In his spare time, he would have been providing ministry to the fighting *Texians* and comforting the families of those who had been lost in battle. He would have performed in excellence as he did in every other endeavor he pursued. There was just something special about Sumner Bacon!

When we look back on Sumner's war effort, it's hard not to see him as a hero. Perhaps he hasn't been recognized as one because he wasn't killed in battle or because he did his best to stay in the background, out of sight, well behind his friend Sam Houston. But the man that bought the cannon powder with his own money and made it possible for the Twin Sisters to fire the first shots of the winning battle, the man who faithfully risked his life as a wartime courier ought to be remembered. At the beginning of 1836, he's an evangelist coming back from a secret mission with a new wife. Six months later he's by my estimation a true Texas hero.

He gave some as apostles, and some as prophets, and some as evangelists, and some as pastors and teachers, for the equipping of the saints for the work of service, to the building up of the body of Christ.

Ephesians 4:11-12

EIGHT: THE MAKING OF THE
TEXAS APOSTLE

Once it seemed the war was at least suspended, Sumner was eager for two really important pursuits in his life. The first was to resume his ministry and the second to finally settle down and get to know his wife. His involvement in the war had been exciting, his almost constant interface with his friend Sam Houston had been rewarding and his travels had made him feel useful even if stressful.

Having been so closely connected to Houston, he knows only too well that the little *Texian Army* has dodged a very large bullet in the immediate aftermath of *The Battle of San Jacinto*. For the time being, it seems clear that the entire Mexican Army has retreated back to Mexico and as long as Santa Anna is in captivity, the consensus is that they probably won't be back right away. In the meantime, thousands of folks are flocking into the new republic wanting to join the Army and help build a nation. But this time they're determined to stay vigilant.

Sumner grieves for the men he'd known personally that had been killed in the war. Because of his courier work, he'd known most of the famous ones like Col. Travis and Davy Crockett and James Fannin. But the one he must have grieved for the most was Col. Jim Bowie because they'd known each other on a personal level before the war and Sumner had shared the gospel more with him than any of the others. Bowie had even protected Sumner a few times and helped his camp meetings succeed. He's prayed for Jim Bowie's soul many times and believes his friend is finally at peace after a life of so much tribulation and disappointment. Sumner remembers all too well that it's been less than three years since Bowie lost his wife and two children to that outbreak of cholera in San Antonio.[79]

Soon the time comes for Sumner to request a release from his Army duties in the late spring of 1836 which General Houston agrees to as long as there's no imminent threat of the war resuming. But Sumner Bacon has no peer as a courier who can be trusted with secret missions to distant places. So, he would have been asked to pledge his speedy return to the side of the general if the war outlook were to change. In fact, about the time he's preparing to leave, Houston asks him to go that second time with a special message to General Dunlap back in Nashville and follow up on the professional militia troops they had previously requested.

As some point Sumner had purchased two hundred acres about six miles east of the town of San Augustine for $750.00 cash.[80] He'd built a nice home there and had recently made his new wife Elizabeth his gracious *Lady of the House.* Two years later they will bring into the world their first of three children: Jonathan in 1838 named after Sumner's father, followed in 1841 by twin girls Mary Ann Chase Bacon and Francis Ellen Bacon, the first twin named after his special friend Benjamin Chase who had been such an important part of his early ministry, in getting appointed by the *American Bible Society* and in his ordination by the Louisiana Synod. The wilderness man who had left his family back in Massachusetts had acquired a new God-given family in Texas.

---

[79] https://en.wikipedia.org/wiki/James_Bowie
    https://tshaonline.org/handbook/online/.../fbo45
[80] "Pistol Packing Preachers" by Barbara Barton, p. 26

Now as Sumner is preparing to resume his ministry, there's a point to again be made about his personal development over the years. At the beginning of his story we found him in a less than prominent family in Massachusetts living on two successive small farms where Sumner's father had trouble being successful in his business dealings. There wasn't enough money for the family to send Sumner to attorney school and the dream died for lack of funding. His older brother followed in the family tradition of failure and so does Sumner for the sixteen years following his departure from Massachusetts. He's a rough-talking, uneducated farm hand and day laborer until he comes into a personal relationship with Jesus at that now famous Presbyterian camp meeting in Arkansas.

Only ten years later he's become a respected, even legendary member of the Texas Protestant clergy with funds enough to buy his own land, buy cannon powder for the Army and cover the cost of building a home. He's also advising leaders at the highest levels of the new republic and making a substantial contribution to the birth of his new nation. The change in him is miraculous. Indeed, his life has become a powerful testimony of what the Holy Spirit can do with a simple believer who's willing to put his/her life fully in God's hands.

Sumner Makes a Change

Historians agree that the focus of Sumner's ministry changes after the war. Before suspending it in early 1835, he'd been a traveling evangelist content to illegally organize Protestant camp meetings and illegally preach the Protestant message and illegally distribute bibles. All that has suddenly become legal and the next generation of preachers can now come in and begin to raise up local community churches and build permanent structures.

The fact is, a new country needs to establish a stable principled culture, and the one that works the best is the one that develops and operates around its churches. Christians need ongoing teaching and discipleship and fellowship and counseling and ministry and moral direction that can only come from established ministries in the setting of the local church. Texas is going to emerge out of its wilderness, frontier ways and more closely resemble the church-centered culture Sumner had known back east. And so, he comes to realize after careful God-seeking and soul-searching, because that's who he is now, that his new job post-war is to help his new republic make this essential transition.

The fact is, Denominational Christianity is exactly what Texas needs in the latter half of 1836 because the denominations are already well-established and can educate and train and certify the clergy that will be needed to raise up the congregations of believers to be the backbone of their new communities. They're also deeply committed to starting newspapers and educational institutions which are desperately needed keeping in mind that the new government is starting off with no money and little structure. Sumner Bacon is in the right place at the right time, a special God-led minister with the commitment and determination to make happen what's most needed in this new Republic. And he's especially looking forward to his newly evolved calling.

According to historians, it had become Sumner's dream to see his beloved *Cumberland Presbyterian Denomination* legally established in the free country of Texas. He'd been waiting for that to come to pass, confident that it would eventually happen.[81] So in the summer of 1836 probably just after his return from his second trip to Nashville, he takes his next step by starting a church in his hometown of San Augustine. A previous Cumberland home church had been established in June of 1833, illegally of course, by Rev. Milton Estill at Shiloh near the town of Clarksville.[82] Now with Sumner's church, there are two Cumberland Presbyterian churches in Texas.

A third church is officially recognized on November 27, 1837 at a meeting in Sumner Bacon's home and it's called the *Watkins Settlement Presbyterian Church*. It had originally started in May 1834 inspired by none other than Sumner Bacon as an illegal home bible fellowship and now becomes a full-fledged church in the key eastern hub town of Nacogdoches.[83] On that same date, Rev. Watkins is ordained in Sumner's home so the church can be recognized. There now being the required minimum number of three Cumberland churches in Texas, Sumner wastes no time in forming the *Texas Presbytery* there on the same date.[84]

It wasn't always easy going to worship in those early Cumberland churches even after they became legal. The following description of the first building that the *Watkins Settlement* members worshipped in, there in Nacogdoches, has been excerpted from a history of the church that was written years later in 1975:

---

[81] http://www.cleburnetimes review.com/news/lifestyles/mike-beard-sumner-bacon-s-mission-in-texas-endures/article_36fb33e0-489b-5a55-bd55-eeda64f816b4.html

[82] http://www.shilohmadrascpc.com/cemeteries

[83] http://www.cumberland.org/hfcpc/churches/RockSpTX.htm

[84] https://tshaonline.org/handbook/online/articles/fba03

It was built of logs and used as a fort also. The actual building was a six-sided log church, with what was described as a "bird-trap" roof of logs covered with boards. The floor and seats were of split oak logs and the door was home-made. The walls had port holes on each of the six sides.

When the members came to church, they stacked their guns in the corners and appointed two sentries to watch out for the Indians. When they saw any Indians coming, they would stick their guns out of the portholes and could tell right away whether they were friendly. Often the Indians came inside the church to listen to the preaching. But when they were on the warpath, the members could get distracted in a hurry. That's because if the Indians had trouble breaking up the services, they might try to throw fire brands on the roof to try to set the church on fire. But, the six sides of the building gave the settlers a good shooting range in all directions and on most days, they were able to hold off the attacks until the service was finished.[85]

It's easy in modern times to lose sight of the hardships early Christian church-goers faced in frontier Texas. Nevertheless, they're determined to assemble together and worship God, seemingly able to overcome any hardship, any obstacle that would keep them away from the worship service. Meanwhile, Sumner Bacon is the principal Presbyterian Leader in the territory traveling around to the various locations, enduring hardships and overcoming danger while encouraging the establishment of new congregations so that growth can continue and the Cumberland denomination firmly grounded.

---

[85] http://www.cumberland.org/hfcpc/churches/RockSpTX.htm

The Texas Synod

By the fall of 1842 there are enough churches raised up so that Sumner can fulfill his dream of forming a Texas *Synod* and at that time a minimum of three presbyteries were required to form one. He had helped raise up the Presbyteries of Texas, Colorado and the Red River and now they're ready to put those three Presbyteries together into the Texas *Synod*. They have their first meeting of the Texas Synod in early 1843 and the Rev. Sumner Bacon is their first Moderator.[86] As you would probably expect, it turns out that this particular group of churches is reported to have taken on the characteristics of its principal founder Sumner Bacon and pursues an especially vigorous evangelistic policy that spreads a network of Cumberland congregations all over the State of Texas by the end of the nineteenth century.

Somewhere around early 1842, Sumner's health begins to fail at the age of 52 and he's not able to travel as much as before. So, he develops a new lifestyle of staying at home with his family, receiving people there for ministry and going out about once a month or so[87] when he feels up to it to go preach someplace, probably the church he had started in St. Augustine since it involved the least amount of travel. In addition to being the force behind the formation of the Texas Synod, he's also somehow found time to start the first temperance society in Texas. But it seems that once his dream has been achieved, his body starts to fail, run down from all the travel and sacrifice and stress he's experienced constantly for more than thirty years.

---

[86] http://www.cumberland.org/hfcpc/minister/BaconS.htm
[87] Ibid

Sumner Bacon's admirable legacy is that his labors were directly responsible for bringing Cumberland Presbyterianism to Texas and for helping establish a firm foundation for it to grow on. And so it was that his contemporaries proclaimed him *The Apostle of Texas* in recognition of his indomitable commitment to spread the gospel across a land of such violent opposition and in recognition also of the importance of his contributions to his Church and to the State of Texas.[88]

The *Apostle of Texas* was a very special man of God doing God's work to help a new nation get started. Without him, things would have most likely turned out a lot different.

---

[88] http://www.cleburnetimes review.com/news/lifestyles/mike-beard-sumner-bacon-s-mission-in-texas-endures/article_36fb33e0-489b-5a55-bd55-eeda64f816b4.html

The time of my departure has come. I have fought the good fight, I have finished the course, I have kept the faith; in the future there is laid up for me the crown of righteousness...

2 Timothy 4:6-8

Well done, good and faithful servant...enter now into the joy of your Lord.

Matthew 25:21

NINE: FINISHING THE COURSE

W hen the Texas Synod was formed in the fall of 1842, Texas is working toward the end of the so-called *Mexican Invasion of 1842* which you can find more about in Appendix Five. All the time that conflict is going on, which was pretty much that entire year, Sumner is working on the formation of his Texas Synod. His deteriorating health doesn't permit him to return to the Army courier service he had so faithfully carried out just six years before. Nevertheless, his passion and commitment to his vision for the Synod keep him occupied and he's able to produce lasting results for the *Cumberlands.*

At that special meeting on November 27, 1842 Sumner Bacon takes his close friend and freshly ordained Pastor Richard O. Watkins aside to tell him privately that with the formation of the Synod his work has been completed and that he won't recover from his illness. Sumner goes on to say that he's had a *presentiment,* in other words a *premonition* that he will soon die.[89]

Had I been the one writing the historical account for the *Cumberlands* about this conversation, I would have called Sumner's comment to Pastor Watkins a "prophetic insight" because God would have been intimately involved in the remaining days of this special minister. It wasn't just some flesh-driven intuitive thing he was relaying to his friend because by connecting it to the idea that his work in the Kingdom had been completed, we can know that Sumner was relaying to Watkins that this was news straight from the Lord.

---

[89] http://www.cumberland.org/hfcpc/minister/BaconS.htm

Fourteen months later on January 24, 1844 just two days after his fifty-fourth birthday Sumner Bacon leaves his home in San Augustine to go to his new home with the Lord.[90] That's a young age even in 1844 for such a vibrant man to be dying. But even with his late start and early death, Sumner has accomplished more than at least ten normal people under the most difficult of circumstances. And I submit by this account of his life and ministry that the name Sumner Bacon should be mentioned alongside the names of our traditional Texas heroes because just as they died and are remembered for their service, Sumner Bacon also gave his life in the performance of extra-ordinary service to his country.

Some years after Sumner's death, Cumberland leaders will write about their great Texas evangelist/apostle. Following is one of the tributes about their special predecessor who came to Texas on his own to do God's work under whatever conditions presented themselves:

"Texas was the field for him, so true it is that when God calls out a workman, he always finds a work suited to the character of him who is thus called. In traversing the wilds of Texas, he preached whenever and wherever an opportunity was offered. He bore a high character of scrupulous honesty, great energy, and punctuality in fulfilling his engagements. Though of a rough exterior and unpolished manners, he had a soul which gleamed with the noblest affections, while he was a stranger to fear. It required a heroic spirit to bear what Protestantism was compelled to bear at that time in Texas. That spirit he possessed in large measure."[91]

---

[90] Ibid
[91] Ibid

I'm fully compelled to faithfully quote verbatim the fore-going description probably written by Cumberland leader Rev. J.B. Renfro because there's no way I could say it any better. The tribute is so well written by such a credible witness that it successfully confirms its own accuracy in portraying a special man that God had personally touched and changed. To leave it out or modify it would have reduced the quality of this publication.

Other testimony on the life of Sumner Bacon included the writings of his friend Rev. Richard Watkins of Nacogdoches who had personally witnessed and been involved in Bacon's work. Years later he wrote the following tribute to his good friend:

"The church that he so faithfully labored to plant in Texas... (now) numbers three Synods in Texas, fourteen Presbyteries and one Presbytery in the Indian country, one hundred and eighty ministers, and more than twenty thousand communicants, with an institution of learning second to none of its age, and a large number of young men of fine promise preparing for the ministry. The labors of this faithful man of God...will tell for the Cumberland Presbyterian Church in the great day of God Almighty."[92]

A modern Cumberland historian wrote so succinctly the following: *"the opening pages of Cumberland Presbyterian history in Texas were indelibly written by one man – Sumner Bacon."[93]*

But Sumner had been given two courses to finish. To be sure, he DID realize his dream for the Texas Synod and

---

[92] Ibid
[93] http://www.cleburnetimes review.com/news/lifestyles/mike-beard-Sumner-bacon-s-mission-in-texas-endures/article_36fb33e0-489b-5a55-bd55-eeda64f816b4.html

upon that achievement a great Protestant denomination was built that contributed mightily to the development of Texas. That was the work he had been sent for and the work he had to complete before he could go Home.

The other course he pursued encompassed the year and a half when he'd suspended his ministry because during that time Sumner Bacon also made a tremendous contribution in the unlikely role of Army courier and personal advisor to General Sam Houston. Think about it for a moment: how is it possible that a recently ordained Cumberland Presbyterian evangelist and bible distributor winds up in the role of assisting the current Commanding Officer of the Army who a few months later will be the President of the new republic? How is it possible that the same evangelist is sent on secret *military* missions to find volunteer troops for the Texas Army and to purchase cannon powder so their new cannons could be fired at *San Jacinto*? Just so you know, those two cannons they fired (the Twin Sisters, see Appendix Three for more information) were the first shots fired and they had the Mexican Army confused and in retreat BEFORE the *Texian* infantry had even moved forward. Just a little factoid so you know how important that famous cannon powder actually was!

To sum it all up, Sumner Bacon arrived in the territory with no credentials to perform illegal ministry and to distribute bibles illegally. He finished that course and became a legendary evangelist in the process. He became involved in the War effort and also finished that course in honor spending his own funds for cannon powder that was used to win the War. And finally, he founded the Texas Synod of the Cumberland Presbyterians and fulfilled his dream to finish the last course. I challenge folks to find a flaw in that resume.

Well done good and faithful servant and thanks be to God for sending us the right person!

If you confess with your mouth Jesus as Lord, and believe in your heart that God raised Him from the dead, you will be saved...

Romans 10:9

TEN: SOME CONCLUDING TAKEAWAYS

This book almost seems to be about two people that both used the same name and claimed to be from Ward, Massachusetts. They were even born on the same day in 1790. But, the first person lived his first 36 years as a less than prominent handy man, in a barely-getting-by kind of lifestyle in the wilderness or as a seasonal farm hand. He was uneducated, had difficulty reading and writing and was reported to be inarticulate except for his expertise at profanity. He had no assets or accomplishments or family to show for those 36 years, no exploits, no business interests, no circle of friends, no reason to think that he would turn out any differently in the remainder of his life than the way he'd performed in the first part. In fact, he was working on a farm in Arkansas as a day-laboring farm hand when everything changed. It was *unlikely*, totally *inauspicious* that he would change, that a different person would suddenly emerge with the same body but with different ways of acting, speaking and working, with a different set of priorities and different goals and objectives and expectations and capabilities. But that's exactly what happened to Sumner Bacon one night down in Arkansas in 1826. One moment he was the original Sumner and an instant later he was a new creation, a different person even though still with the name Sumner Bacon.

There's only one way this could've happened. People just don't otherwise change so suddenly and so profoundly and so completely. But under the right circumstances, the change will always happen to anybody on earth if they want it to and are willing to fulfill the simple requirements. The change may not be as outwardly pronounced as it was for Sumner but there WILL be the same change inwardly. I know this because the Bible tells me so and I believe that every word in the Bible is divinely inspired truth. Also, I know it's true because it happened to me the same way and because thousands of people have told me independently and personally that it happened to them too.

Without getting too technical about it, what the Bible actually says is that every person ever born on the earth has started out from birth with a predisposition to sin. God didn't originally create us that way but we've chosen to disobey Him and go in the wrong direction. We can't help it. We just sin even if we don't want to.

But sin is offensive to God, so in time He brought onto the earth His own Son whose Name is Jesus and who lived a perfect life for thirty-three years without sinning so that by the shedding of His blood, He could pay for all the sins of all mankind for all time. Had those sins not been paid for, then mankind would have been condemned to be separated from God for eternity. Fortunately, because of what Jesus accomplished, God has already forgiven mankind for all sin for all time: past, present and future so we won't have to stay separated from Him.

But there's one thing we each have to do to take advantage of this arrangement: we have to believe. By believing we automatically receive God's forgiveness which is exactly what Sumner Bacon did that night down in Arkansas: he simply believed and asked Jesus to come into his life. The Bible says that the moment he did that, the moment he decided to believe, he was changed and a new reborn Sumner Bacon emerged with new qualities and new abilities even though he continued living in the same body.

Where before he was fearful, he was now fearless. Where before he was inarticulate, he became eloquent and persuasive. Where before he'd had no purpose or vision for his life, he became purpose driven and fully aware of God's plan for his life. Where before he'd been unsuccessful and mired in hardships, he became successful and overcame his hardships. Where before he'd been financially strapped, he became a man of substance with wisdom and effective decision-making. The new Sumner was a new creation, a man entirely different than the old Sumner.

Perhaps as you read this, you're wishing that you could make the same change. Like Sumner Bacon you've gotten to a point in your life where you're tired of the old ways of defeat and you want to let God change you into the person you've always wanted to be that coincidentally God made you to be. There is within you a desire, a longing to be the person God designed you to be and truthfully the only thing holding you back from realizing that potential is giving your life to Jesus. The only thing it takes to change to a new creation is to believe.

If you've never invited Jesus to be your Lord, you can do so by simply believing and saying out loud something like the following simple prayer:

Jesus, I declare with all my heart that I believe in you and I believe that God raised you from the dead. I acknowledge that my sins have been forgiven for all time and I ask you to come into my life and be my Lord and Savior. Thank you for salvation and eternal life.

If you were sincere as you prayed, God has already come into your life and you're a new creation, a totally new species recreated in His image. Now ask the Lord to lead you to a good faith-based, bible-teaching church where you can be equipped to fulfill your potential in the Kingdom of God.

Also, when you get a moment, have someone help you look up the following Bible scriptures because they confirm what you've done by saying this prayer and believing what you said:

Romans 10:9
2 Corinthians 5:17
Ephesians 2:8

Sometimes it's hard to accept the idea that the Bible is telling us the truth about God when we haven't read it yet. How could you put your confidence in something you haven't read, that you don't know anything about? Most people start out that way and come to understand it later after they've read through it a few times. You see, before they believe, most people come to a point in their lives when they're so desperate and lonely for God they make their decision *hoping* that it's true, *hoping* that God will show up to start changing things for them.

In the story of Sumner Bacon, we have his testimony, his actual experiences to show us clearly that God _will_ show up. If He showed up for Sumner, He'll show up for you too. The only way to explain the change that occurred in his life is that God showed up and started changing things. People aren't capable of making that much change on their own. It's only possible with God and He loves you just as much as He loves Sumner Bacon. I guarantee you this: God will show up for you if you ask Him to and He will take over.

Truthfully, that's all there is to it and it explains why Sumner Bacon was able to change so quickly, so dramatically and so completely after that night in Arkansas. May God bless you from the reading of this little book and cause your life to change to something you never dreamed possible!

APPENDIX ONE:

FIVE UNCOMMON SETTLERS

Five Uncommon Settlers

*The following articles have been included as they originally appeared in the publication: **The Influence of Christianity on Early Texas History**. Used by permission.*

Now there are certain of the settlers in Texas history that have to be specially mentioned even though their names aren't usually brought up in a discussion about Christian influence. On the surface, these five famous men seemingly had little to do with religion but they <u>did</u> have a profound impact on Texas history and wound up changing the religious environment entirely.

They came to Texas with the great influx of settlers between 1820 and 1836, each one trying to sort out some special issues in his personal life, hoping to regain some lost ground and wanting to find a new life just like everybody else. No matter what happened in their lives before they came to Texas, they're remembered today as heroes, perhaps larger in death than they were in life although they were pretty big in life too. And one thing they did do, which maybe wasn't high on their personal list of priorities but happened anyway, was to help make a way for freedom of religion in what was to become the Republic of Texas.

Stephen F. Austin

Stephen Fuller Austin has been called the founder of Anglo-American Texas and eventually the *Father* of Texas.

 He was born in southwestern Virginia in 1793 and came to Texas in 1820 after his business failed in Missouri. He became the first of the "settler impresarios" when he contracted with the Mexican authorities to bring at least 300 families into Texas in 1821 in exchange for special land grants. He had complete civil and military authority over his colonists until 1828, subject only to nominal supervision from Mexican officials in San Antonio and Monterrey.

Austin's contemporaries largely disagreed with his rather cautious policy of continually conciliating those officials instead of standing up more strongly for their growing list of demands which of course included among other things the relaxation of the Catholic-only rule. The settlers accused him of weakness and instability but criticism didn't cause him to abandon his strategies. The fact is had he not taken this approach, rebellion would probably have erupted before the settlers were ready and set back independence for decades.

In 1834, Stephen F. Austin was finally able to arrange for a measure of religious tolerance with a new state law providing that no person should be molested on account of religious or political opinion if he didn't disturb public order. And, even though he had stubbornly opposed the growing call for revolution, Austin eventually supported the cause for a new republic when he saw that the revolution was inevitable. His support was a key step toward what was to soon follow and he became the first

Secretary of State of the new republic. Unfortunately, he soon died at age 43 on December 27, 1836.

Samuel Houston

Sam Houston was born on March 2, 1793 near Lexington, Virginia. From 1813 to 1814 he fought in the Creek War and was wounded at Horseshoe Bend. He was elected to  the U.S. Congress in 1823 and again in 1825. In 1827 he became the governor of Tennessee. In 1832 after a failed marriage and a bit of a rough lifestyle, Houston moved to the Mexican territory of Texas where he was soon a prominent voice in pushing for secession from Mexico. As tensions mounted, Houston accepted an appointment to command a ragtag Texan army against the Mexican forces who were intent on putting down all rebellious elements.

Sam Houston though soon showed he was a brilliant military leader. He was presented with a particular opportunity on April 21, 1836. Outnumbered by a better equipped Mexican army, Houston noticed that the Mexican General _Antonio López de Santa Anna_ had "for some reason" decided to split his forces. Seeing his chance Houston ordered the attack on the contingent at _San Jacinto_ and his decisive victory secured for Texas its independence in a matter of a couple of a few hours.

Sam Houston became the Texas George Washington. The city of Houston was named in his honor in 1836, and that same year the newly christened Lone Star Republic elected him as its president. After Texas joined the United States in 1845, Houston served as a U.S. Senator until 1860. Following the outbreak of the Civil War, Houston, who'd been elected governor of Texas, refused to pledge his allegiance to the Confederate States of America and an infuriated Texas legislature discharged him of his duties. He died on July 26, 1863 in Huntsville, Texas.

William B. Travis

William Barret Travis was the Texas commander at the battle of the *Alamo*. He was born in Saluda County, South Carolina on August 9, 1809 and came to Texas after

 abandoning his wife, son and unborn daughter in Claiborne, Alabama because he believed his wife had been unfaithful and that he was not the father of her unborn child. As the story goes, he killed a man over that situation and left for Texas where he arrived in 1831 as <u>an illegal alien</u>. He was illegal because the *Mexican Law of April 6, 1830* among other things had specifically banned any further immigration of Anglo settlers into the Texas territory. But that didn't stop Travis and he arrived in San Felipe de Austin and obtained land from impresario Stephen Austin.

He soon established a legal practice in Anahuac, a significant port of entry located on the eastern end of Galveston Bay. The purpose of the move there was to establish himself in an area where there were few

attorneys while he learned Spanish the official language. From his base in Anahuac he traveled around the territory doing legal work and soon became associated with a group of militants who opposed the *Law of April 6, 1830*. Eventually this group became known as the War Party as tensions increased between the Mexican government and American settlers. Travis bounced around from skirmish to skirmish and was regarded by many Texans of the day as a trouble maker. Eventually he was branded an "outlaw" by the Mexican military authority in San Antonio. In January 1836 he accepted a commission as a lieutenant colonel in the Texas cavalry and became the chief recruiting officer for the Texas militia.

His appointment to that assignment soon took him to the Alamo the very next month where he died by a single gunshot to the head after a couple of days of fighting. As history would have it, the nature of Travis's death elevated him from a mere commander of an obscure garrison to a genuine hero of Texas history.

David Crockett

David Crockett was born in Greene County, East Tennessee on August 17, 1786. Between 1813 and 1821 he pursued a military career in various capacities and locations and was appointed or elected to several local township political positions. In August 1821 he took a big step up by running for a seat in the Tennessee legislature which he won. From that time forward he took an active interest in public land policy for the West. In 1827 he was elected to the U.S. House of Representatives, re-elected in 1829 and proceeded to split with President Andrew

Jackson and the Tennessee delegation on several issues including land reform and the Indian removal bill. In his 1831 campaign for a third term, Crockett openly and

loudly attacked Jackson's policies and was defeated in a close election.

As David's fame grew, he won re-election to Congress in 1833 but lost again in 1835 as his political split with Andrew Jackson grew deeper. Disenchanted with the political process and with his former constituents, David decided to do what he had famously threatened to do on several occasions: *"explore Texas and move his family there if the prospects were pleasing."* On November 1, 1835 he departed for the West with three other men and according to his statements he had no intention of getting into the fight for Texas independence. He arrived in <u>Nacogdoches</u>, Texas in early January 1836 and it didn't take long for him to change his mind about getting involved in the swiftly developing battle with Mexico.

The split with Andrew Jackson proved again to be a life-altering event because David made a fateful decision based on it. General Sam Houston had ordered William Travis to abandon the Alamo but Travis deliberately disregarded him. David had a decision to make when he got to San Antonio: he could either join up with General Houston or with Travis in the Alamo. Sam Houston was an Andrew Jackson supporter so David Crockett chose to go to the Alamo. And of course, along with many other heroes, he died there on March 6, 1836 after living in Texas for a total of two months: short time, big impact.

James Bowie

James Bowie was born in Logan County, Kentucky on March 10, 1796 and became a well-known pioneer, soldier, smuggler, slave trader, and land speculator. Like

many frontiersmen of the day, Bowie became intrigued by the idea of Texas, so he moved here in 1830 apparently one step ahead of his creditors back in Louisiana. In short order he found plenty to keep him busy including: 1) a land speculation scheme, 2) a victorious defense against a Tawakoni Indian attack while 3) looking for a particular silver mine he had heard about and 4) the charms of the Senorita _Ursula Veramendi_, the well-connected daughter of the mayor/vice governor of San Antonio. His fame and reputation as a tough frontiersman grew rapidly and in 1831, he married Ursula and took up residence in San Antonio. Unfortunately, she and her parents soon died tragically of cholera.

In the following years Bowie became actively involved in the independence movement and was responsible for several skirmish victories. But ultimately, to make a long story short, he made the bad decision to also disobey Sam Houston's orders to demolish and abandon the old Alamo Mission in San Antonio and sought instead to fortify it and make a defense. After all, San Antonio had become his home town.

When William Travis eventually arrived on the scene, there was strife between the two over which of them would lead the fortification. But David Crockett the experienced politician soon arrived and was able to diffuse things helped by the fact that Bowie became debilitated by a sudden illness. History says that James Bowie was killed on his sick pallet firing his pistols at the enemy when the Mexican army overran the Alamo on March 6, 1836.

James Bowie was another of the rough and tumble settlers that came to Texas to seek their destinies. He came here with his Bowie knife in hand, the same one he first used in 1827 to kill a rival, and he became in death an unlikely hero, one of the five special heroes that have captured the imagination of succeeding generations of Texans since that day in the Alamo. *"Remember the Alamo"* became part of the war-cry for the Texas army that attacked Santa Ana at *San Jacinto* and won the independence from Mexico the settlers had wanted. These were five special settlers that will never be forgotten and the independence they helped win produced freedom of religion for the people of Texas.

APPENDIX TWO:

TEXAS DECLARATION OF INDEPENDENCE

The text of the declaration is followed by the names of the document's sixty signers
in the style they actually signed the document:

UNANIMOUS
DECLARATION OF INDEPENDENCE,
BY THE
DELEGATES OF THE PEOPLE OF TEXAS,
IN GENERAL CONVENTION,
AT THE TOWN OF WASHINGTON,
ON THE SECOND DAY OF MARCH, 1836

When a government has ceased to protect the lives, liberty and property
of the people from whom its legitimate powers are derived, and for the
advancement of whose happiness it was instituted; and so far from
being a guarantee for the enjoyment of those inestimable and
inalienable rights, becomes an instrument in the hands of evil rulers
for their oppression; when the Federal Republican Constitution of their
country, which they have sworn to support, no longer has a substantial
existence, and the whole nature of their government has been forcibly
changed without their consent, from a restricted federative republic,
composed of sovereign states, to a consolidated central military
despotism, in which every interest is disregarded but that of the army
and the priesthood – both the eternal enemies of civil liberty, and the
ever-ready minions of power, and the usual instruments of tyrants;
When long after the spirit of the Constitution has departed, moderation
is at length, so far lost, by those in power that even the semblance of
freedom is removed, and the forms, themselves, of the constitution
discontinued; and so far from their petitions and remonstrances being
regarded, the agents who bear them are thrown into dungeons; and
mercenary armies sent forth to force a new government upon them at
the point of the bayonet. When in consequence of such acts of
malfeasance and abdication, on the part of the government, anarchy
prevails, and civil society is dissolved into its original elements: In such
a crisis, the first law of nature, the right of self-preservation – the
inherent and inalienable right of the people to appeal to first principles
and take their political affairs into their own hands in extreme cases –
enjoins it as a right towards themselves and a sacred obligation to their
posterity, to abolish such government and create another in its stead,

calculated to rescue them from impending dangers, and to secure their future welfare and happiness.

Nations, as well as individuals, are amenable for their acts to the public opinion of mankind. A statement of a part of our grievances is, therefore, submitted to an impartial world, in justification of the hazardous but unavoidable step now taken of severing our political connection with the Mexican people, and assuming an independent attitude among the nations of the earth.

The Mexican government, by its colonization laws, invited and induced the Anglo-American population of Texas to colonize its wilderness under the pledged faith of a written constitution, that they should continue to enjoy that constitutional liberty and republican government to which they had been habituated in the land of their birth, the United States of America. In this expectation they have been cruelly disappointed, inasmuch as the Mexican nation has acquiesced in the late changes made in the government by General Antonio Lopez de Santa Anna, who, having overturned the constitution of his country, now offers us the cruel alternative either to abandon our homes, acquired by so many privations, or submit to the most intolerable of all tyranny, the combined despotism of the sword and the priesthood.

It has sacrificed our welfare to the state of Coahuila, by which our interests have been continually depressed, through a jealous and partial course of legislation carried on at a far distant seat of government, by a hostile majority, in an unknown tongue; and this too, notwithstanding we have petitioned in the humblest terms, for the establishment of a separate state government, and have, in accordance with the provisions of the national constitution, presented the general Congress, a republican constitution which was without just cause contemptuously rejected.

It incarcerated in a dungeon, for a long time, one of our citizens, for no other cause but a zealous endeavor to procure the acceptance of our constitution and the establishment of a state government.

It has failed and refused to secure on a firm basis, the right of trial by jury; that palladium of civil liberty, and only safe guarantee for the life, liberty, and property of the citizen.

It has failed to establish any public system of education, although possessed of almost boundless resources (the public domain) and, although, it is an axiom, in political science, that unless a people are educated and enlightened it is idle to expect the continuance of civil liberty, or the capacity for self-government.

It has suffered the military commandants stationed among us to exercise arbitrary acts of oppression and tyranny; thus trampling upon the most sacred rights of the citizen and rendering the military superior to the civil power.

It has dissolved by force of arms, the state Congress of Coahuila and Texas, and obliged our representatives to fly for their lives from the seat of government; thus depriving us of the fundamental political right of representation.

It has demanded the surrender of a number of our citizens, and ordered military detachments to seize and carry them into the Interior for trial; in contempt of the civil authorities, and in defiance of the laws and constitution.

It has made piratical attacks upon our commerce; by commissioning foreign desperadoes, and authorizing them to seize our vessels, and convey the property of our citizens to far distant ports of confiscation.

It denies us the right of worshipping the Almighty according to the dictates of our own consciences, by the support of a national religion calculated to promote the temporal interests of its human functionaries rather than the glory of the true and living God.

It has demanded us to deliver up our arms; which are essential to our defense, the rightful property of freemen, and formidable only to tyrannical governments.

It has invaded our country, both by sea and by land, with intent to lay waste our territory and drive us from our homes; and has now a large mercenary army advancing to carry on against us a war of extermination.

It has, through its emissaries, incited the merciless savage, with the tomahawk and scalping knife, to massacre the inhabitants of our defenseless frontiers. It hath been, during the whole time of our connection with it, the contemptible sport and victim of successive military revolutions and hath continually exhibited every characteristic of a weak, corrupt and tyrannical government.

These, and other grievances, were patiently borne by the people of Texas until they reached that point at which forbearance ceases to be a virtue. We then took up arms in defense of the national constitution. We appealed to our Mexican brethren for assistance. Our appeal has been made in vain. Though months have elapsed, no sympathetic response has yet been heard from the Interior. We are, therefore, forced to the melancholy conclusion that the Mexican people have acquiesced in the destruction of their liberty, and the substitution therefor of a military government – that they are unfit to be free and incapable of self-government.

The necessity of self-preservation, therefore, now decrees our eternal political separation.

We, therefore, the delegates, with plenary powers, of the people of Texas, in solemn convention assembled, appealing to a candid world for the necessities of our condition, do hereby resolve and DECLARE that our political connection with the Mexican nation has forever ended; and that the people of Texas do now constitute a FREE, SOVEREIGN and INDEPENDENT REPUBLIC, and are fully invested with all the rights and attributes which properly belong to the independent nations; and, conscious of the rectitude of our intentions, we fearlessly and confidently commit the issue to the decision of the Supreme Arbiter of the destinies of nations.

RICHARD ELLIS, president of the convention and Delegate from Red River.

B. Stewart

Thos Barnett

John S.D. Byrom

Charles Fran^{co} Ruiz

J. Antonio Navarro

Jesse B. Badgett

Wm D. Lacey

William Menefee

Jno Fisher

Mathew Caldwell

William Mottley

Lorenzo de Zavala

Stephen H. Everitt

Geo W. Smyth

Elijah Stapp

Claiborne West

Wm B. Scates

M.B. Menard

A.B. Hardin

J.W. Bunton

Thos J. Gasley

R. M. Coleman

Sterling C. Robertson

Benj. Briggs Goodrich

G.W. Barnett

James G. Swisher

Jesse Grimes

S. Rhoads Fisher

John W. Moore

John W. Bower

Saml A. Maverick from Bejar

Sam P. Carson

A. Briscoe

J.B. Woods

Ja^s Collinsworth

Edwin Waller

Asa Brigham

Geo. C. Childress

Bailey Hardeman

Rob. Potter

Thomas Jefferson Rusk

Chas. S. Taylor

John S. Roberts

Robert Hamilton

Collin McKinney

Albert H. Latimer

James Power

Sam Houston ◀◀

David Thomas

Edwd Conrad

Martin Parmer

Edwin O. LeGrand

Stephen W. Blount

Ja^s Gaines

Wm Clark, Jr.

Sydney O. Penington

Wm Carrol Crawford

Jno Turner

Test. H.S. Kimble, Secretary

APPENDIX THREE:

THE STORY OF THE TWIN SISTERS

THE STORY OF THE TWIN SISTERS

The following Appendix has been included in this publication because the "Twin Sisters" cannons were instrumental in the Battle of San Jacinto and the powder that fired them had been purchased in New Orleans by the Rev. Sumner Bacon with his own funds in the amount of $561.00. The Twin Sisters are a precious part of Texas history.

On November 17, 1835, after Francis Smith *(an agent sent by the Texas Provisional Government)* [94] convinced the people *(selected business people)*[95] of Cincinnati, Ohio, to aid the cause of the Texas Revolution, the Ohioans began raising funds to procure two cannons and their attendant equipment for Texas. Since the United States was taking an official stance of neutrality toward the rebellion in Texas, the citizens of Cincinnati referred to their cannon as "hollow ware" *(which would have appeared on all of the various shipping documents instead of referring specifically to "cannons" – author's note).*

Two guns, probably six pounders, were manufactured at the foundry of *Greenwood and Webb* in Cincinnati and then shipped down the Mississippi to New Orleans. William Bryan, an agent of the Republic of Texas in New Orleans, took official possession of the guns on March 16, 1836. *(Sumner Bacon would have been in New Orleans at about that same time to purchase cannon powder – author's note).*

From New Orleans the guns were placed on the schooner *Pennsylvania* and taken to Galveston Island. For some reason they were not accompanied by their limbers and ammunition, perhaps because the dangerous military

---

[94] http://earlytexashistory.com/Twin%20Sisters/TS%20Web/TS%20one.html
[95] Ibid

situation in the republic did not allow for any delays *(or because of the U.S. official policy of neutrality – author's note)*. The cannons arrived in Galveston at the beginning of April 1836. On board the *Pennsylvania* was the family of Dr. Charles Rice, who was moving to Texas. Upon arrival in Galveston the guns were presented to representatives of Texas under the sponsorship of Dr. Rice's twin daughters, Elizabeth and Eleanor. Someone in the crowd made notice of the fact that there were two sets of twins in the presentation, the girls and the guns, and thus the cannons became the *Twin Sisters*.

After several unsuccessful attempts to get the *Twin Sisters* to the Texas army under Sam Houston, which was retreating toward the Sabine before the forces of Gen. Antonio López de Santa Anna, the Twins finally reached the army on April 11, 1836. A thirty-man artillery "corps" was immediately formed to service the guns, the only artillery with the Texas army, and placed under the command of Lt. Col. James Clinton Neill.

Only nine days later the Twin Sisters saw their first action during a skirmish between the armies of Houston and Santa Anna on April 20. In this fight Neill was wounded, and command of the guns passed to George W. Hockley. The next day, April 21, 1836, saw the battle of San Jacinto and the securing of fame for the Twin Sisters.

That afternoon near the banks of Buffalo Bayou the Texas army struck at Santa Anna's unsuspecting troops. The Twins were probably near the center of the Texans' line of battle and ten yards in advance of the infantry. Their first shots were fired at a distance of 200 yards, and their fire was credited with helping to throw the Mexican force into confusion and significantly aiding the infantry attack.

During this battle the Twins fired hand-fuls of musket balls, broken glass, and horseshoes, as this was the only ammunition the Texans had for the guns.

On April 21, 1841, they were fired in celebration of the fifth anniversary of the battle of San Jacinto. When Sam Houston was inaugurated as president of the republic that year, the twins were fired as Houston kissed the Bible after taking the oath of office.

Author's Addition: After the Sam Houston celebratory firings, the cannons were scrapped and wound up in Louisiana where they were eventually found and reconditioned for service toward the end of the Civil War. After that no one knows where they went but to this day historians are still looking for them.

The foregoing Appendix is a partial article made available on the Internet by the Texas State Historical Association, Handbook of Texas Online, Jeffrey William Hunt, "Twin Sisters," uploaded on June 15, 2010, modified on March 8, 2011, published by the Texas State Historical Association. The information has been quoted verbatim with occasional additional comments by the author of this book.

This material has been used in accordance with Title 17 U.S.C. Section 107 related to Copyright and "Fair Use" for Non-Profit educational institutions, which permits Make A Way Ministries, to utilize copyrighted materials to further scholarship, education, and inform the public. As a nonprofit Christian teaching organization, Make A Way Ministries makes every effort to conform to the principles of fair use and to comply with copyright law.

APPENDIX FOUR:

SANTA ANNA'S CAPITIVITY

SANTA ANNA'S CAPTIVITY[96]

 When Santa Anna approached Houston after the Battle of San Jacinto, General Houston was lying wounded under a large oak tree. A short dialogue ensued. El Presidente Santa Anna threw himself on Houston's mercy, advising that since Houston had conquered and captured the Napoleon of the West, he could afford to be merciful. After negotiations Santa Anna sent a dispatch to the rest of the Mexican Army in Texas:

"I have agreed with General Houston for an armistice (peace treaty) and the war will cease forever."

Two treaties were prepared for Santa Anna, known as the treaties of Velasco. A public treaty which stated:

"All hostilities will cease, and Santa Anna would not cause arms to be taken up against the people of Texas."

The secret treaty stated:

"That El Presidente should be sent home at once to Vera Cruz, Mexico and that he would prepare things in Mexico so that a commission sent by the Texas government should be received, and that by means of negotiations all differences between Texas and Mexico should be settled and independence of Texas acknowledged. The Rio Grande was agreed upon as the boundary."

These bargains arranged, El Presidente embarked on a schooner named the *Invincible* at the mouth of the Brazos on June 3, 1836, bound for Vera Cruz. He was quite happy at

---

[96] Excerpted from "The Life of Santa Anna" by Clarence Wharton, 1926; see also, http://www.tamu.edu/faculty/ccbn/dewitt/santaanna4.htm

having traded these treaties for his life, and issued a happy farewell address to the Texas people. There was a tremendous outcry in Texas at this time for Santa Anna's execution, and the provisional government had great difficulty in keeping order. A few hours before the schooner sailed, a ship came into the Brazos from New Orleans, bearing a company of soldiers from the United States for the war in Texas. After the news of San Jacinto's outcome was spread to the U.S. there was rush of adventurous people who wanted to participate in the war, and these newcomers determined that the Mexican President should be kept in Texas. They defied the provisional government, and boarded the *Invincible* before it could set sail, and forcibly took possession of El Presidente with the purpose of having him tried and shot. He was taken up the Brazos river to the Phelps plantation, about 30 miles from Velasco, and kept there during the summer and autumn.

A rumor was spread that an attempt was to be made to rescue him, and indeed such a plan was in progress, and he was put in irons and chained to a live oak tree. Santa Anna's imprisonment under these circumstances weighed so heavily upon him that he became melancholy.

The first congress of the Republic of Texas assembled at Columbia on the Brazos in October, and the fate of the captive president was a great question on which was debated in both houses. The leaders in congress were in favor for his execution, and if the matter had been left to a vote, he would no doubt have lost.

But General Houston, who had been elected President of Texas in September, 1836, had determined that to spare his life was the right thing to do. Andrew Jackson, President of the United States, had written Houston, urging that he be released. In November, while the congressmen at Columbia were debating the fate of the "illustrious prisoner," President Houston cut the debate short by deciding to send him to Washington with an escort. Well-armed, the escort party and Santa Anna left the Brazos on the 25th of November, 1836, and rode toward the Lynchburg crossing of the San Jacinto, and near the sunset hour on a November day they rode across the battlefield. El Presidente turned and cast a long and remorseful look at the scene of his greatest disaster.

Santa Anna did not want to go to New Orleans, for the Texan spirit of revolution was so strong there that he feared for his life, and they rode through northern Louisiana to the Mississippi River, where they took a passing steamboat up the Mississippi to the Ohio, and up the latter river to Louisville, Ky., which place they reached on Christmas day, 1836. News that the Mexican president was passing through the country excited lively interest, and crowds were gathered at each stopping place for a look at him. Everywhere he was treated with the utmost courtesy and curiosity.

In Washington, he visited President Jackson. The real story of Santa Anna's trip to Washington has never been widely known. There was a fight in the American Congress, upon the recognition of Texas' independence. Jackson's administration was coming to a close and he was to be succeeded the following March by Martin Van Buren who was very conservative about the recognition of Texas, or any other act that would bring on war with Mexico.

President Houston of Texas thought that it would help the situation if Santa Anna would go in person to Washington and say to President Andrew Jackson that Mexico did not intend to make an effort to reconquer Texas. This would be an answer to the critics in Congress who were urging that the recognition of Texas would be considered an unfriendly act by Mexico. Because of this guarantee Jackson was able to recognize Texas. It was one of the conditions of Santa Anna's release that he should do this, and though he was supposed to be freed when he left Texas under an escort, in fact he was still a prisoner until he left Washington.

He carried out his part of the bargain and in private conversations with President Jackson gave the message that he had been sent to deliver and this was a powerful aid to the recognition of Texas which was accomplished during the last hours of the Jackson administration. Santa Anna was speedily as possible set sail for home. He was sent to Vera Cruz on the United States frigate *Pioneer*, as the guest of the American Navy.

El Presidente landed at Vera Cruz on his return from Washington and the Texas campaign on February 23, 1837, an absence of a little more than one year, and went direct to his plantation, where he announced his retirement from public life.

While he was away, his old enemy, Bustamente [sic], whom he had overthrown and sent into exile in 1832, had returned, and in June, 1837, while Santa Anna was at his plantation, Bustamente was elected President of Mexico for a five-year term. Santa Anna remained on his plantation for the next two years, planning a return to power and overthrowing Bustamente once again.

The foregoing excerpts have been reproduced as originally written including the original grammar, punctuation and misspellings. The new President of Mexico in 1837 was Anastasio Bustamante.

APPENDIX FIVE:

THE MEXICAN INVASION OF 1842

THE MEXICAN INVASION OF 1842

The following account has been excerpted and quoted from the below resource, occasionally edited to provide additional clarification as necessary: **http://www.forttumbleweed.net/invasion.html.**

During the early days of the Republic of Texas, there was constant tension over the possibility of a Mexican invasion. Then in January of 1842, General Mariano Arista issued a statement from Monterrey telling the *Texians* that it was hopeless for them to continue their struggle for independence and promising amnesty and protection to all who remained neutral during his planned invasion.

The Mexican army then invaded Texas and by early March of 1842, the Mexican army occupied Goliad, Refugio, and Victoria. This caused a panic in San Antonio and the Texas army retreated leaving San Antonio unprotected and soon occupied by the Mexican army.

On March 10, President Sam Houston declared a national emergency and ordered the republic archives to be moved to Houston, but the people of Austin refused to let the records go resulting in (what came to be called) *The Archive War*.

President Houston then called out the Texas militia (under Alexander Somervell) on the 15th of March 1842 to fight the invaders but by now, the Mexican Army had already retreated toward Mexico. A major result of the March raid into Texas caused widespread panic in the western settlements of the Republic of Texas as they realized their vulnerability to the Mexican army.

The young Republic of Texas was strapped for cash so President Houston made an appeal to the United States for money and volunteers. An army was raised but not funded and the army was dismissed by June of 1842.

On September 11, 1842, Mexican Gen. Adrián Woll, with a force of 1,200 Mexicans, recaptured San Antonio. In a few days, over 200 Texan volunteers gathered on Cibolo Creek above Seguin and marched to Salado Creek about six miles northeast of San Antonio. On September 18, Caldwell who was in charge of the Texas troops, sent Hays and a company of scouts to draw the Mexicans into a fight which was known as the battle of Salado Creek. While the battle of Salado Creek was raging, Capt. Nicholas M. Dawson approached from the east with a company of fifty-three men. These men were attacked a mile and a half from the scene of the battle and killed in what came to be known as *The Dawson Massacre*.

The Mier Expedition

Mexican Gen. Woll drew his Mexican army back to San Antonio and then hastily retreated to Mexico pursued by the smaller Texas force. However, the Texans returned to San Antonio without engaging the Mexican troops and joined up with a larger force that became known as the *Mier expedition*.

The *Mier Expedition* of approximately 300 men elected William S. Fisher as their commander and moved down the Rio Grande (River) opposite the Mexican town of Mier.

Fisher and the Texan forces crossed the river on December 23, 1842 and occupied the town of Mier without opposition. They vacated later that day, after the town leaders promised to deliver supplies to the Texan camp.

This action was thwarted by Mexican General Pedro Ampudia and his troops who prevented the attempted delivery of supplies. The Texans then re-entered Mier on Christmas day and heavy fighting broke out.

Although the Texans were outnumbered by ten to one, they make a good account of themselves killing over 600 Mexican troops and wounding another 200 while suffering only 31 men killed or wounded. Then the Texans ran out of rations and soon agreed to a surrender. The Texas prisoners were held in the town of Matamoros and then moved to Mexico City. During the forced march, (many of the) captured Texans escaped and all but three were recaptured before they could get back to Texas.

The Black Bean Episode

The recaptured Texans were sentenced to death by Mexican dictator Antonio Lopez de Santa Anna but the order was later reduced to 10% of the men to be executed as determined by lottery. In the lottery, which came to be known as the *Black Bean Episode*, 17 of the Texas prisoners who drew black beans from a jar were blindfolded and shot.

The remaining prisoners were marched to Mexico City, where they spent the summer of 1843 making road repairs. In September, they were transferred to *Perote Prison*, a highly secure stone fortress East of Mexico City. Here, they either died, escaped or remained until the last of the group was released on September 14, 1844.

The remains of the men executed in the *Black Bean Episode* were returned from Mexico in 1848 during the Mexican War and buried at *Monument Hill* near La Grange, Texas beside the victims of *The Dawson Massacre* of 1842.

Bibliography

http://www.forttumbleweed.net/invasion.html

Archie P. McDonald, Travis (Austin: Jenkins, 1976).
William Barret Travis, Diary, ed. Robert E. Davis (Waco: Texian Press, 1966).
Amelia W. Williams, A Critical Study of the Siege of the Alamo and of the Personnel of Its Defenders (Ph.D. dissertation, University of Texas, 1931.
Report: Southwestern Historical Quarterly 36 [April 1933], 37 [July, October 1933, January, April 1934).

Author's Comments

There are several reasons for including this information in this book. The first is that the incidents of 1842 occurred almost at the end of Sumner Bacon's life and he wasn't able to participate in them due to bad health. Undoubtedly, he would have wanted to be a part of it because it was a *major* invasion by an old enemy and there was still great animosity in the new Republic from the conflict in 1836. It was also a violation of Santa Anna's three treaties and his personal assurances to President Andrew Jackson in 1837 that he would refrain from these kinds of provocations. True to form, he was never one to let his word get in the way of self-interest. But, his misguided strategy of frequently harassing the Texas Republic wound up driving it into the U.S. in 1845 as the 28th State and ultimately involved his country in a devastating war with the U.S. where they were decisively defeated losing all the rest of their western territory above the *Rio Grande River* all the way out to California.

A second reason to include it is that most Texans aren't aware of this later invasion when we study our history and yet it lasted for most of 1842 involving the Republic in an armed disruption of the peace and loss of life in addition to the expenditure of scarce funds. It lasted longer than the original War of 1835-36, but fortunately the *Texians* were more prepared than in 1836 so it was a fruitless exercise that caused Mexico another defeat and more animosity from their neighbors to the north.

The final reason for including this incident is to show once again that Santa Anna was a military man who on occasion lacked honor in his determination to demonstrate to the people to his north his bitterness for their having caused his defeat at San Jacinto. To execute captured military people by bean lottery was a serious abuse of human life and added fuel to the fire of the difficult relationship that has existed between Mexico and Texas for almost two hundred years.

So, What Did You Think of the Book?

First of all, thanks for purchasing it. I know you could have picked any number of books to read, but you picked this one and I'm really grateful.

I hope it added value to your life and helped you develop a more complete biblical perspective. If so, it would be really helpful if you would please share this book with your friends and family by posting your positive comments on Facebook, Twitter and other social media. We really appreciate your help!

Also, if you enjoyed the book and believe the message needs to get out to as many people as possible, please take a few moments to post a review on Amazon. Just go to this link:

https://www.amazon.com/gp/product/1725799065/ref=d bs_a_def_rwt_bibl_vppi_i1

I want you to know that your review is very important for the Body of Christ. It will raise our rankings with Amazon which will make it possible for more people to see it and find out what the Bible actually says about our borders.

If you aren't sure how to make a review, the next page goes into a little more detail. Come and be a part of this important ministry. May God especially bless you for making this extra effort!

How to Write and Submit a Review

Writing a review on Amazon is really easy. Just go to the book's front page and under the heading Customer Reviews, you will see a button for writing a review. Click on it and you will be taken to a page set up for 'Your Reviews' where you can write reviews for your purchases.

What you do is:

1. Select the **rating** of the book from 1-5 stars, with 5 being the best score.

2. Write your **book description** in the box provided. Keep in mind that if you leave this page before submitting your review, you'll have to start over again. I would recommend writing the review first in Word or Evernote and then copy and paste.

3. **Create a headline** for the review.

4. Hit **submit**. Your review will go live within a couple of hours, although it could take up to 24 hours.

One point to be clear about here is that according to Amazon's policy for posting reviews, you have to have an account that has **made a purchase of at least $50** using a valid credit or debit card.

ABOUT THE AUTHOR

Dr. Bill Miller is an ordained cross-denominational minister, elder-at-large and founder of a national nonprofit Christian organization called *Make A Way Ministries*. He has been involved in financial counseling and teaching since 1985 and has assisted tens of thousands of families to overcome financial problems and get on to financial success and victory.

He also pastored the bilingual (English/Spanish) *Faith Life Fellowship Church* in Miami Florida from 2007 until 2012.

Dr. Miller has published a bible-based e-newsletter called *Prosperous Life Newsletter* since January 1998 and has written more than 25 books and e-books about various financial topics with the purpose of helping families overcome financial problems on a practical level.

This publication connecting Christianity to Texas History is his second effort outside the financial arena and he has promised there will be more to come. He's happy to say to anybody who'll listen: *"We need to know more about what God was doing when all that Texas history we celebrate was being formed. Jesus is a Texas Hero too!"*

Dr. Bill was born in Houston, Texas a long time ago and is a graduate of *Texas Tech University* in Lubbock. He also holds a Doctorate in Ministry from *Miami Christian University*. He currently lives happily and works busily with his wife Sherri carrying out their ministry in the special historic community of Granbury, Texas.

Thanks for reading this book. We hope it blessed you and that it helped strengthen your personal relationship with Jesus Christ.

CPSIA information can be obtained
at www.ICGtesting.com
Printed in the USA
BVHW051017220123
656836BV00014B/532

9 781536 962864